Managing Working
with the Public

LOCAL GOVERNMENT MANGEMENT SERIES

This series provides local government managers with the help required to understand the rapidly changing context in which they work. The current pressures on managers, created by the changing public expectation of services and the policy and budgetary framework, require a major expansion of their responsibilities and make more demands on their know-how and skills. The books will guide these managers through the processes of the practical handling of increasingly complex management tasks and issues. Valuable insights into successful management practice and a sound understanding of the local government context are combined to enable first-level managers and above to fulfill their new role effectively and efficiently.

SERIES EDITORS

The series editors have both been senior managers in local government. **Paul Corrigan** has worked in economic development at the GLC, been Deputy Director of ILEA's educational social work services and was Head of Quality Management at the London Borough of Islington. He was lead consultant in the establishment of the Camden Education Department. In recent years he has worked as a management consultant in local government. **Paul Joyce** was employed as Chief Training Officer and Assistant Director of Personnel at the London Borough of Islington in the early 1990s. He is now Director of the Management Research Centre at the University of North London. Both editors have been involved in research on the management of local government, both being interested in applied research which is of use to those with responsibility for the success and effectiveness of local government.

MANAGING IN LOCAL GOVERNMENT SERIES

Managing Working with the Public

Edited by
SUE GOSS

PUBLISHED IN ASSOCIATION WITH THE
IDeA IMPROVEMENT AND DEVELOPMENT AGENCY

KOGAN
PAGE

First published in 1999

Kogan Page Limited
120 Pentonville Road
London N1 9JN

British Library Cataloguing in Publication Data

A CIP record for this book is available from the British Library.
ISBN 0 7494 2973 9

Typeset by Kogan Page
Printed and bound by Clays Ltd, St Ives plc

Contents

List of figures

List of tables

List of contributors

All the contributors are part of a multi-disciplinary team at the Office for Public Management, an independent centre developing management practice and thinking in the delivery of public services.

Anne Bennett is an occupational and organizational psychologist with a background in research and consultancy with the Cabinet Office, and across central government and the wider public services. She has developed and run a series of 'Vision' events at the Office for Public Management.

Robin Clarke designs and runs deliberative consultation events such as citizens juries and community workshops. Before joining the Office he worked as a consultant in community engagement specializing in local government and health research. Previously he worked as a researcher for an MP.

Claire Cowley has particular experience in quantitative research. Before joining the Office she worked as a research officer at City of York Council. Prior to this, Claire worked for three years at MORI, specializing in local government research.

Sue Goss is Director of Public Services Development at the Office for Public Management. She has been a public sector consultant for many years, and has written and researched widely on issues of public management and community engagement. Previous publications include *The Changing Role of Councillors* (with Paul Corrigan), *Civic Entrepreneurship* (with Charlie Ledbeater), *The Future Role of the Chief Executive* (OPM), *Councils in Conflict* (MacMillan) and *Local Labour and Local Government* (Edinburgh University Press).

Jon Harvey specializes in whole organization quality. With a background in psychology, Jon had many years' experience of training executives, managers and front-line staff.

Loraine Martins has extensive experience of working in the fields of community relations, equal opportunities, racial harassment and policing. She works with public organizations, voluntary organizations and local communities.

Clive Miller has many years' experience in strategic inter-agency work and community involvement. His previous career involves work as senior consultant at the National Institute for Social Work. Clive has written widely on user engagement and social inclusion.

Kai Rudat is a research and consultation specialist and is the Director of the Office's Stakeholder Engagement Unit. Prior to joining the Office, he was Director of Health and Social Research at MORI and a researcher and broadcaster for the BBC World Service.

Paul Tarplett has worked in both private and public sector organizations and has led human resource management and training in large private sector companies. He has special expertise in organizational development and change. He is the author of *Managing Strategy* (with Greg Parston, OPM).

Acknowledgements

We would like to thank all who have provided the background material for this book. In particular, we would like to thank Dave Allen and Carole Dixon, at the City of York Council, Stella Clarke and Irene Kszyk of the Policy and Equalities Unit at Lewisham Council and Alison Barlow for help with the chapter on surveys and panels, and Kennet District Council and Barnsley Metropolitan Borough for case studies on 'delighting the customer'. We would like to thank all our clients and colleagues in local government and at the Office for Public Management who have contributed to the analysis in this book. We are also grateful to Charles Lesley of the Improvement and Development Agency (I&DeA) for his comments on the book.

Introduction

Sue Goss

Public services will change radically over the next five to ten years. The biggest change is likely to be a different relationship with customers, the public and local communities. We argue in this book that there is an opportunity to rethink, alongside the public and communities we serve, the way we do things – and to find new sorts of services for the 21st century. By seizing these opportunities, as well as tackling the practical difficulties, it is possible to draw on an emerging range of methods and approaches in order to 'manage working with the public' in ways that meet local needs and objectives.

There are many examples of good practice set out in this book and in other excellent guides (see 'Further reading' at the end of the book). Chapter 2 concentrates on working with the public, which is an integral part of the new agenda, and essential to achieving 'best value' and 'Beacon status'. However, many hard-pressed managers in local councils experience the demand to consult as another 'external pressure'. They have often experienced poor consultation, and are sceptical about its value. In this book we show not only how to overcome the problems and pitfalls, but how to ensure that 'working with the public' adds value.

The reality is that the speed of change is making old ways obsolete. Among the changes needed will be a change in the way local government managers think about our relationship with customers and citizens. While we have experimented with public engagement for a decade, change has been painfully slow. Closer working with local people may offer solutions to previously intractable problems.

Local authorities need to collaborate with many other agencies if they are to succeed in meeting local aspirations, for example with police and health authorities, private companies, and charities and voluntary organizations. Collaborative and partnership working are important themes throughout this series of books. In this book, however, we concentrate on the relationships local authorities need to build with local people, as service users, as citizens and as co-producers of local solutions to local problems.

This book is not simply a theoretical or academic account of public and user engagement. My colleagues and I at the Office for Public Management have spent 10 years working alongside public sector managers to make 'managing working with the public' a practical reality. During this time we have drawn on tried and trusted methods and approaches, but we have also developed new ones. We have worked with local authorities, health authorities, police authorities and other bodies to set up panels, surveys, citizens' juries and focus groups. However, we have also developed deliberative processes, visioning workshops, open space events, open negotiation workshops – approaches tailored to meet the specific situations we find in particular localities. We have watched things go wrong in a hundred interesting ways, but we have also begun to see things go right; to see sustained processes of shared working that achieve measurable results. Each chapter reflects a different area of exploration, but forms part of a collective journey, one which we have been attempting to share in practice with managers, politicians and local communities. This book is, therefore, a useful summary of a collaborative effort, drawing on the particular expertise of a number of colleagues, and attempts to chart a path through current thinking and practice, and future development.

We are convinced that managing with the public is the only way forward. However, our practice in the field has been driven by the need to find practical answers to three problems described over and over again by local government managers – problems we set out below to act as a 'frame' for the rest of the book:

1. 'MANAGING WITH THE PUBLIC IS PROVING MORE DIFFICULT THAN WE THOUGHT'

Managing with the public is tough. Some managers love the challenge of radical thinking and enjoy the informality of working with the public, but many experience public engagement as tricky and uncomfortable. Managers and politicians have to listen to unwelcome criticism, without much in the way of support or reassurance about what is going right. For managers and councillors who experience the daily grind of juggling competing claims with shrinking resources, hearing about more public needs and wants simply adds to their problems. New ideas and suggestions are frustrating if there are not the mechanisms in place to implement change. People in the community are often equally frustrated, and can be rude and belligerent. Hard-working managers can simply experience consultation as pointless extra work, or as a process of being bullied by members of the public! Old-fashioned methods often make this worse, creating an adversarial atmosphere. Even when mutual understanding is good, there are no simple answers. Different sections of the community want different things, and we cannot always deliver what people want.

2. 'THE PUBLIC DO NOT REALLY WANT TO BE INVOLVED'

There is no evidence that shows that the public do not really want to be involved. Indeed, the evidence we have (PMF, 1997) indicates that they do, when we take it seriously. However, they do not want to be involved if it means turning out on a wet Wednesday, sitting on hard chairs in a draughty community centre, and listening to a load of middle-aged men droning on from the platform in dense jargon. Nor if it means spoiling the family dinner to fill in a long questionnaire about things that do not seem important. There are 'professional participators' who like meetings and have a passionate interest in something. There are some political activists from all shades of political opinion who take their citizenship very seriously, and are articulate and confident in public meetings. However, for most people, too many evenings spent talking to 'suits' from the council would be a warning to 'get a life'.

Most people have young children, aging parents, long working hours, poor transport, hobbies, love affairs, films, discos, pubs and friends, to fill their busy lives. Indeed, it is extraordinary that so many people do make the effort to get involved in local affairs in spite of how boring, inaccessible and frustrating we often make the process. Attending council and public meetings and forums responding to draft documents, are all activities that require very high levels of motivation, prior knowledge, skill and confidence. No wonder they only attract very few people. They are structured in ways that meet our needs, but ignore the needs or interests of the public.

This is dangerous. It is dangerous because it accelerates the public's disengagement with local democracy. More and more people feel that it is irrelevant to their lives. It means that we fail to communicate. It means that our services are provided and organized with only the vaguest of ideas about how they are experienced.

3. 'WE DO NOT HAVE ENOUGH MONEY TO PROVIDE BASIC SERVICES, SO WHY WASTE MONEY ASKING PEOPLE ABOUT THEM?'

Good public engagement costs money. It uses up scarce resources that could be used to provide services. However, we know that the public welcome consultation and believe that there is not enough. Without effective engagement, we may spend money on the wrong things and make the wrong choices – we may be ineffective in meeting community aspirations.

Creating solutions

Throughout this book, we explore ways to tackle these problems. A useful first step is not to see it as the council's job to 'solve' the problems raised, but to share 'solution-finding' as well as 'problem-finding' with the community. It is also clear that if we are to make public engagement work, we have to help to change our organizations. If we try to 'bolt on' fashionable consultation techniques to old ways of doing things, we simply exhaust ourselves. We have to learn and change, and enable people in our communities to learn and change. We have to relish the experience of learning from mistakes. Things go wrong continually – people do not turn up, consultation yields only vague replies, councillors take decisions that contradict public opinion, communities fall out with each other, feedback is muddled and action does not follow. However, the practical process of encountering and tackling these problems is what equips us to cope with the more interesting problems that we are likely to encounter in the future. We need to develop a certain sense of comfort in managing within complex situations, in juggling competing interests and in cobbling together agreement about next steps that are neither neat, nor polished.

We have discovered the importance of paying careful attention to potential audiences. If people are not interested, then we have failed to make it interesting. We have probably failed to engage people in discussing their own problems, and tried instead to make people interested in our problems. Throughout this book, therefore, we have tried to draw attention to some of the more imaginative ways to engage the public – the use of improvizations, video-boxes, Internet chat-lines, youth conferences, visioning events, negotiation workshops and consensus conferences.

If we need people to engage then we should make it easy, stimulating and useful. We should try to make citizenship fun to exercise. The most successful processes do not just 'take' information from the public, but give something back – an opportunity to learn new skills, to make friends and to find out how to access services. Ordinary members of the public can develop their own capacity to think strategically, to innovate and to discuss and plan action. It may help people to get work, or training, to make useful contacts, to develop confidence and self-discipline. Some techniques are simply pleasurable, for example experiments with theatre or cartoons.

Case study: Animation project for Chinese women, Liverpool; Liverpool City Council, Education Directorate, in partnership with Jackdaw Media and the Chinese Pagoda Community Centre

Educational Opportunities Initiative (EOI) was an innovative adult education research and development project, funded by local and central government funding streams. Its project team undertook an action research study which highlighted the Chinese community's need for link-skills programmes (especially IT). As a way to engage Chinese women in the services provided by their local community centre, and to help them overcome their techno fear by introducing them to state-of-the-art equipment used in the world of animation, EOI co-ordinated a multi-agency programme which resulted in an animation short course, utilizing the specialist skills of a local women's film group, Jackdaw Media. The group was commercially successful (having been short-listed for various awards and sold footage to the regional TV network) and was located in the Chinese community, but had very little contact with it. Using the Pagoda Community Centre as the site for weekly workshops, these two groups of women came together to design and then animate their work. Enthusiasm was such that women took their work home, where their children helped. This also encouraged a culture whereby mothers and children bonded to do homework together. The Merseyside Chinese Youth Orchestra offered to play and record a soundtrack for the video. The animated film, highlighting themes of cultural harmony, was subtitled in English and Cantonese, and was used as a training aid.

We also need to make good use of common sense. We need to use resources sparingly, and efficiently. We should not 'waste' consultation; we should always be prepared to act effectively in response. We should not duplicate effort, or gather more information if we have not yet acted on what we already know. We should target carefully, and focus effort in areas where the maximum impact can be achieved. We need to treat public engagement with all the rigor of evaluation and assessment that we would apply to other aspects of our work. Did it work? What would success look like? Have we developed an approach that is 'fit for purpose'?

More importantly, we should not see public engagement as something that goes on outside the 'day job'. It is not necessary to set up a huge and complicated process of consultation. It may be more important to translate engagement throughout the culture of daily work; receiving feedback from service users, discussing their comments, enabling front-line staff constantly to update managers and councillors about views, perspectives and problems; using complaints and daily feedback to guide management action; and using existing events and forums to gather additional information, sharing skills, knowledge and information with the community. There are a hundred ways that 'managing with the public' can be threaded through daily work.

Many managers feel lost in the emerging jargon of community engagement, the deluge of 'good practice' advice, and the ever-increasing range of methods and approaches. However, it is not method that is at the core of effective public engagement, but mindset. Unless we understand, and agree with the reasons for engaging with the public in new ways, we are unlikely to make them successful. That is why this book not only discusses some very important methods of public consultation but places them within the real managerial practice of local government managers. They have to play a vital role in making those choices.

Chapter outline

Chapter 1 concentrates on some of the different purposes and logic behind public engagement, and argues that a number of parallel changes in politics, lifestyles, technology and attitudes make old ways unsustainable. It explores the extent to which different reasons for engagement lead us to adopt different approaches. Ultimately, the answer to the question 'Why engage?' will be different for different authorities and departments and managers. However, if there is no powerful logic driving a process of consultation or engagement, it will fail.

Managing with the public is not a complicated science to be understood only by experts. There is knowledge to be acquired about different methods, about the problems that can arise and how to tackle them, but this should become as much a matter of course as basic knowledge about managing people or budgets. There are important skills – listening, negotiating, facilitating and balancing – but these will increasingly become core skills in local government. More important is a set of attitudes and behaviours that seeks out and values the contribution of local people; that welcomes question and challenge; that copes with complexity, contradiction or confusion within and between communities, and is able to seize opportunities to change services rapidly in response. Perhaps the most important competence to be acquired is that of deciding what sort of approach makes sense locally, and in creating the right environment within which engagement will succeed.

Chapter 2 explores the range of different methods and approaches that are available, and develops a vocabulary which can help to make good decisions about which approach to use. It maps out current approaches on a series of dimensions based on different stages of consultation; on different sorts of legitimacy; on different sorts of audience and on a spectrum from opinion to judgement. It looks at other factors, such as geography, scale, resources and organizational readiness, and offers a rough-and-ready guide to a comprehensive set of options. A summary is contained in the section 'Brief guide to different methods for managing working with the public' in Chapter 2.

Chapter 3 begins a process of exploring some of the key methods of consultation and engagement in depth. Claire Cowley looks at surveys and panels, and at the issues and practical problems to be addressed. Robin Clarke in Chapter 4 looks at deliberative methods. In Chapter 5, Jon Harvey explores the specific issues around customer care policies, and responsiveness to customer needs.

Anne Bennett in Chapter 6 introduces the range of new techniques that are being developed around community visioning, and suggests that processes that engage the wider community in identifying problems and issues also contribute to a wider ownership of possible solutions.

Chapter 7 examines the implications for the changing relationship between managers and politicians, and explores the changing roles of politicians, and the changing nature of local democracy. It sets out some practical steps to be taken if managers and politicians are to work effectively with each other, as well as with the public.

In Chapter 8, Loraine Martins and Clive Miller examine the contribution that public engagement can make to social inclusion; the issues that need to be taken into account when working with people who have traditionally been excluded from decision-making, and ways to create empowering processes.

In Chapter 9, Paul Tarplett examines the problems encountered inside the organization once 'managing with the public' becomes a reality, and looks at the implications for organizational culture, and for the skills and competencies that individual managers need. Finally, Chapter 10 looks ahead to the future, and attempts to outline possible future trends.

How to use this book

It is not necessary to read through the whole book starting from the beginning. You may be only interested in particular chapters or in certain sorts of technique. It is designed to be dipped into and to offer practical help at many different stages.

In each chapter we have included case studies and 'tasks' which can be used to help reflection or which can be used as a starting point for explanation with your teams at work.

1 The reasons for change

Sue Goss

INTRODUCTION

We argue throughout this book that closer working with local people offers new solutions to previously intractable problems. This chapter attempts to examine changes in the wider society and the role of local authorities that makes this change necessary. It argues that engaging with the public has become a core activity for public managers.

NEW GOVERNMENT AGENDA

In 1997, the new Labour Government swept to power with a large majority, and a modernizing agenda for local government. In the 1980s and 1990s the agenda was focused on efficiency and competition. This will be no less important in the future, but there is a new and equivalent focus on effectiveness and accountability.

Through discussion documents, guidance, legislation and new monitoring arrangements the government has shown that it is determined to modernize local democracy. The reforms it is planning to introduce include a change to the political structures introducing elected majors and executive cabinets, innovations to increase the proportion of people who vote at local elections, a new best value regime to replace Compulsory Competitive Tendering (CCT), new powers for partnership and a new general duty to promote the social economic and environmental well-being of the area. At the heart of many of these policies is a determination to make government more accountable to local people, and the recent Green Papers spelt out the new approach to consulting local people, suggesting that local authorities consider setting up panels and focus groups, citizens juries and referenda to get closer to local people.

The government's proposals for best value are not simply about making services more efficient. Local authorities will be required to consult local people and businesses about the services they provide, set targets for improvement and report back to local people. The effectiveness of consultation will be assessed alongside the quality of the services provided. While there will still be a place for well-designed surveys, and effective consultative forums, these will increasingly coexist with emerging approaches to consultation that promote dialogue with a wide cross-section of the community. If consultation processes are truly to enable local authorities to engage with increasingly diverse local communities, local government managers will need to find methods that match the complexity of the task.

There is a new focus on outcomes, at central and local government level. The Social Exclusion Unit, for example, has set out outcome targets for the 44 most deprived districts in the country to bring levels of crime, education, training and health closer to the national average. Government indicators and targets are increasingly phrased on outcome terms, for example 'the educational attainment of looked-after children in the care of social services'. Local councils are setting themselves goals which focus attention not on processes, or systems, but on the quality of life of local people, cutting unemployment, for example, or developing sustainable communities on local estates.

'The Modernising Government' White Paper stresses the need for all public agencies to work across boundaries to deliver new solutions to social problems by pooling the resources, staff knowledge and energy of a number of agencies to create fresh thinking and challenge professional boundaries. Cross-boundary thinking has made possible new approaches to youth justice, to regeneration to sustainable development and to social exclusion. Government messages are sometimes mixed, but if the government stresses outcomes, rather than simply compliance with government instructions, the hope is that local government and other agencies will be empowered to look outwards rather than inwards. New performance measures are evolving that concentrate on the effectiveness of government agencies' contribution to improving the lives of local people, rather than on professional procedures and demarcations.

Running through all aspects of the 'modernization agenda' is a new approach to consulting, and engaging local people. Indeed, the Improvement and Development Agency (I&DeA) has developed a model of the capabilities of a successful council which includes effective consultation as one of the three most important elements.

So perhaps the most obvious answer to the question 'why engage?' is 'because we are going to have to'. The government's powerful system of penalties and rewards, from best value to 'Beacon status', will be geared to rewarding authorities that engage successfully, and penalizing those that do not.

However, while government 'sticks' and 'carrots' are important, they are not the most important determinant of local action. The experience of the last

10 years has shown how easy it is for local authority managers to give the appearance of following government guidelines while carrying on much as before. The drivers for change are more profound, and the government is as much a follower as a leader – responding to major upheavals in social and economic life. Much of local government has already woken up to these changes, and will be innovating far ahead of the government agenda. Legislation will only create a baseline below which local authorities cannot fall. Far-sighted local government managers will recognize the wider and longer-term pressures for change, and plan accordingly.

CHANGING ATTITUDES TO LOCAL SERVICES

It is clear that public attitudes to local government services are changing; not everywhere, and not at the same speed in all sections of the community. There are still places where expectations are very low, and the assumptions of a traditional paternalistic state are still in place. There remains considerable bedrock support for the welfare state, for education and the health service in particular. However, recent surveys and consultation exercises among young people, more mobile people and the better off, show that they see local government as becoming less and less relevant to their lives. The public expects and demands that local government services change with the times.

It helps to look at some history. Many services provided by local government are recognizable as services provided at the end of the 19th century – for example public baths, libraries, welfare services – although many are new, and some of the early services such as health, have passed to national level. In the early years, councils were small, and spending was relatively low, but councils were free to spend the product of local rates as they chose. As services grew, increasing proportions were paid for by central government grants. Local government was reorganized in 1963/4 in London and in 1973/4 in the rest of the country to replace a relatively chaotic set of municipalities – many quite small – with a supposedly more coherent and streamlined two-tier system, with district councils responsible for most local services and county councils responsible for strategic planning, education, social services and transport strategy. In the 1960s and 1970s, local government was seen as a primary service provider and was considered a success.

The cracks began to appear in the mid-1970s. The tower blocks and new housing estates of the 1960s began to develop design problems, and life in these new estates turned out to be little better than it had been in the slums they replaced. It turned out that big was not as beautiful as had been thought. Public services were seen as bureaucratic, inefficient and clumsy. The

Thatcher Government swept to power in part because it harnessed popular anger about the failures of an expensive public sector to deliver good quality services.

The Conservative Government response to the perceived inefficiency of public services was to draw on what was seen as the dynamism of the private sector to 'shake up' public provision. New systems were introduced: performance management, quality assurance and unit costings – public organizations learnt how to calculate their inputs and count their outputs. Local authorities, subject to CCT and to repeated cuts and freezes in funding, became more efficient, and in many places public sector services increased in quality, if not in quantity.

Nevertheless, local authorities have found it harder and harder to grapple with local problems. They have less and less control over resources, and a sense of shrinking power. Constant budget trimming meant that services often failed to meet local needs; school performance in the inner cities was poor; and social services fell far short of demand and offered little choice. Voting in local elections has declined, and surveys show that local people understand less and less about local politics. So, for councillors and managers in many councils, particularly in the inner cities, a new relationship with citizens and consumers has been seen as a crucial part of any strategy to tackle local problems. The last 10 years have seen, alongside the efficiency savings, attempts to build more consultative and more open relationships with local people. The new government initiatives build on, and draw lessons from, much of that innovative practice.

 Task

Gather all the data that your local authority has about what the public think about your local authority. At various times in the book this will be an important resource.

First, simply gathering all the data may be very hard because departments will have been carrying out their own consultation exercise. The housing department will have consulted tenants in order to develop its housing strategy. The social services department will have consulted a wide range of different groups for its community care plan and the education department will have consulted schools, governors and parents in order to fulfil its obligation to write an education development plan.

THE PRIVATE SECTOR REVOLUTION

The rest of society has continued to change, at an ever increasing rate. The economy has become increasingly global, with customers able to access goods and services from all over the world. We can order books from the USA, buy airline tickets from a call-centre in Calcutta and get advice via the Internet from Australia. The public has become used to constant service innovation, vast choice and products tailored to very specific customer segments – clothes, hobbies, gardening, music, food, interior design – have become divided into tiny, fast moving niche markets. More and more services are accessible through the telephone, or through computers, for those of us who are technology literate. The Internet gives access to information, news and advice from all over the world. Indeed, a new social division is beginning to open up, between the technologically rich, and the technologically poor.

Private sector companies are changing how they organize the work process. Companies have experimented with many different structures from huge corporations to small and flexible units, with experiments in matrix, federal and network structures. Increasingly, people work from home using new technology. New sorts of skills are needed and valued, and new management paradigms for the new millennium.

 Task

Compare the way in which you personally carry out your private finance with bank, insurance company and mortgage with how you carry out your public finance – council tax and income tax.

 Task

Ring up five local building societies and hear how they immediately introduce themselves to you.

Now do the same with your own local authority, local secondary school, hospital and swimming baths.

Are they similar in their response?

CHANGING COMMUNITIES

Polling evidence shows that people value the idea of community as highly as ever, but its meaning has changed. Communities are fragmenting. They are not simply geographically located – close networks of friends can be spread across a whole city – and they are not homogeneous. The ethnic diversity in our cities that offers a wide range of businesses, shops, restaurants and neighbourhoods also means that the histories, attitudes and needs of local people are equally diverse. The difference between urban and rural life is striking. Old people live very different lives from young people, and the links between them are weakening. Many people are still vulnerable in our society, and without the help they need, but the old 'one size fits all' solutions do not work.

Lifestyles are diverging. We can watch one of a dozen TV channels, graze through 20 radio stations, find pubs, restaurants and leisure activities tailored very specifically to our age, income range and lifestyle choices. People see their community not as a geographical space, but as a grouping of people with similar interests or problems.

At the same time as there is all this private choice, there is a widening of inequality. More families live in relative poverty than they did in the 1970s. Even among the comfortably off, there is increasing public anxiety about things that we cannot control on our own – pollution, traffic congestion, pesticides in food, BSE and about financial futures. We may enjoy low taxes, but we all experience the downside of greater inequality and public squalor, as fear of crime begins to rise and young kids with no hope of work are tempted into drugs and violence. A section of the community, especially the young unemployed, have become less and less engaged with civic society and, therefore, less likely to vote or value social cohesion. Public services could, if change does not take place, cease to be part of a unifying civic culture, and become simply residual provision for those who cannot afford to buy privately. The rich, as much as the poor, have become a separate subculture, living in mock Georgian mansions behind security gates.

The information society – the end of professional 'expertise'

The public has more information from which to make their own judgements. They are better informed about public affairs, and the introduction of performance measurement helps them to assess the relative quality of local services. School league tables and measures of clinical effectiveness have equipped people with more information with which to challenge professional judgements.

This contributes to a sense that professionals – once revered as experts by a socially deferential society – are not foolproof. Ordinary people have begun to distrust and to challenge the judgements of professionals. The failure of many professionals to communicate well, or to keep up with the times has exacerbated a rapid loss of trust in their judgements. It is not that the public has lost respect for professional judgement – it is that the public expects professionals to listen to and respect their judgements as well.

Professionals can no longer rely on 'knowing best'. Professional training has often been based on building up a body of theory which can be drawn upon in a particular case. However, as we increasingly see the complexity of the world around us it becomes clear (as perhaps it always should) that no single profession has the experience to tackle multiple social problems.

Implications for local government

The reality of all these changes is that old local government ways of doing things cannot survive. The changes taking place in the wider community and in government mean that local authorities have to become far better at listening, at finding out about changing lifestyles, needs and choices, and at engaging people in the decisions to be taken. This does not mean endless vague consultation exercises – it means carefully designed and targeted dialogue that takes place in ways that make sense to local people.

Drivers for change

- new government agenda;
- focus on outcomes;
- current resources stretched to the limit;
- more articulate, more information-rich public – higher expectations;
- community fragmentation;
- more private choice;
- less faith in professionals.

COMMUNITY PLANNING

Because of the multiplicity of pressures for change there is a need for local choices about user engagement. Individual managers and management teams will have a lot to think about, and to balance, when choosing when, how much and how to engage the public. Precisely because there is little agreement about 'the right way', and because all the pressures conflict, there is much to think about.

We all have experience of change undertaken under compulsion, especially from government. Local managers have become experts in 'rebadging' current activity using the new buzz-words, in filling in application forms to try and attract funds by redescribing things in new ways to press important policy 'buttons'. We all have business plans, strategies and service plans, but it is not clear that very much really changes. We sometimes just go through the motions.

However, when we are dealing with public consultation, this is not simply a waste of time, it is positively harmful. Consultation exercises undertaken under compulsion tend to be vague and dull. The people who participate feel undervalued and become irritated by the lack of feedback or action. Ineffective consultation, with no commitment to act on what has been heard, breeds cynicism and apathy. It makes it harder to engage with local people in the future. It can cost a lot of money, and only leads to a fat report that no one reads. Unless the managers responsible for consultation on the ground understand and share the objectives for consultation the danger of going through a purely cosmetic exercise is high.

At the same time, we know that services are often stretched to breaking point. Few users of services would be supportive if they were told that their library or swimming pool had been closed to finance consultation! Resources are limited, and should not be squandered. Good consultation requires investment, but it also requires that that investment pays off. There is a need for both common sense and a best value approach to consultation.

Service effectiveness

If services are to become more effective, in many circumstances, the *status quo* is not an option. Even when current services work smoothly and well, we may need to think again. There may be duplication between different agencies. We may use bureaucratic processes that are outdated; services may not be user-friendly; or it may just be that new technology or innovation by competitors has created better ways to do things.

All authorities, even if they are locally satisfied with services, will have, under best value, to review them all, to explore whether they still meet their objectives and whether they could be delivered in better ways. Understanding user views will be an important part of this. Best value will only work well as a process to support continuous improvement if user and public views are used to help investigate and diagnose problems and build alternative solutions, to examine assumptions and rethink delivery options.

This does not mean that expensive or comprehensive options are necessarily the best. The right approach may be to do something small scale effectively and well, and to learn the lessons before embarking on a vast consultation project. The next chapter explores an approach to choosing different methods in more detail.

The most important question to ask is always – 'Why?' Why are we doing this? Without a clear answer to the 'why' question, it is hard to set a strategy. And then 'How?' How are we going to do this? How do we know it works? The views and experiences of local people are one of the most powerful sources of evidence about whether or not our services are working well.

Engagement with the public is not limited to feedback on the provision of services. Local authorities have an important role in representing local communities; and to do that well they must understand their views, priorities and perceptions. Since we know that the public do not all think the same way, local government managers need ways to understand the differences, and the problems and dilemmas that face different groups of citizens.

Community planning offers a process for engaging with the whole community to identify the right goals for the local authority. These may not be limited to service provision – many local authorities have adopted goals that match community needs but are outside their direct responsibility – to reduce unemployment, reduce crime, tackle the problems of young people and reduce pollution. There is scope to engage the public directly in the work of new partnerships.

However, to be effective, community planning needs to go beyond the 'articulate' and the well organized. Some of the most exciting examples of neighbourhood planning show what can be done. Community planning opens the way to radical and innovative approaches to community engagement; to the use of video, theatre, open-space events, community visioning and consensus conferences. New technology can contribute to new deliberative methods. It becomes possible to bring together people from different sections of society to hear from each other, and begin to negotiate through solutions rather than expecting the councillors to solve everything from the centre. The potential is considerable and we are only just beginning to tap it.

We will explore in later chapters some of the new approaches to community engagement that offer opportunities to extend community planning and decision-making to a much wider section of the community.

Case study: London Borough of Islington

The London Borough of Islington launched its community planning process by involving about 90 local stakeholders and residents in developing a vision of how they wanted Islington to be – exploring ways of living and working in the future that they would value. Key themes emerged around transport, the environment and accessible services. The outputs were recorded on video and photographs, and the materials generated by the groups were used as an exhibition in the community museum as a first step to getting further feedback.

Case study: Sandwell Metropolitan Borough

Sandwell Metropolitan Borough has started to develop a corporate community plan with the express aim of creating 'a thriving, sustainable and forward-looking community by 2010'. The plan is to build a civic partnership, made up of approximately nine local organizations, to focus on the long-term objectives for the area. The community plan will guide the action of the local authority, and be used to integrate other corporate and service agendas. In order to reflect bottom-up input from the community, the 'vision' for Sandwell will be created on the basis of a widespread community/partnership consultation process. Consultation is planned in three stages:

1. *Public consultation*   This involves the leafleting of every household in Sandwell and inviting community groups to contribute to the vision.
2. *Voluntary sector/business sector consultation*   This involves asking local business leaders and umbrella organizations to contribute, as well as setting up strategic forums to promote further debate.
3. *Agency consultation*   This involves inviting a wide range of public and private sector agencies to contribute to the debate and shed light on particular aspects of the vision, such as its impact on health, environmental and educational issues.

DEVELOPING LOCAL REASONS FOR USER ENGAGEMENT

Unless you are clear about the reasons for the choices you are making you are unlikely to choose the right approach, nor to implement it sufficiently well to achieve your objectives.

These choices will match your wider social objectives. Setting clear and measurable goals for consultation is an important first step. These may be set at corporate level, and we would always suggest a process of discussion involving all managers and staff across the authority to share objectives, understand strategy and ensure that the approaches chosen seem workable to everyone. If they are not explored corporately, then objectives for consultation will probably be set within departments, business units, Best Value teams or cross-cutting project teams. Whoever is responsible, it is important to ensure that they are aligned with the overall goals of the authority.

✎ Task

Think through the most recent consultation exercise engaged in by your section or your department. Was there a clear objective at the start of the process? Did managers choose from a range of methods the way in which they consulted the public? Were the managers aware of how they might implement any proposals that spring from the consultation before it started?

We set out below a number of reasons for engaging with the public or with service users. No doubt there are more, but they may help to clarify why the council wants to engage with local people, and to make sure that it is successful in achieving the objectives that have been set. In the next chapter, we explore ways of choosing the method that matches these reasons.

Enlightened self-interest – improving the message

A common reason for consultation is to win support for a policy the council wants to pursue. The primary objective is, therefore, to explain the policy and to build understanding of what the council is trying to achieve; this is a communication rather than a consultation exercise. The council has to communicate the right messages to the right people and even when the objective is to persuade others, listening is as important as telling.

It is sometimes assumed that simply communicating does not count as consultation and is not, therefore, as important as other approaches (Pollitt, 1988). However, research carried out as part of the 'best value' evaluation process by the University of Warwick shows how important good communication is as a baseline for any consultation. Their study in the pilot areas showed that 41 per cent of respondents felt that their council 'is too remote and impersonal'. A poll showed that local councils were considered the worst communicators by far, compared with a wide range of agencies, including British Telecom (the best), local schools, British Gas, Inland Revenue and the DSS! (DETR, 1999). There is considerable evidence that local people are confused by local government. They do not know who provides their services and how they can access them and do not know to whom to complain when services do not meet their expectations. Without basic information, other forms of consultation and communication cannot work.

Understanding the local community

It is important to understand the needs, priorities, problems and aspirations of local people. That seems obvious, but it is often not easy to see past the vocal campaigners, to understand the viewpoints of all sections of the community. The growth of partnership working has created opportunities to pool information and statistics, to identify 'hot-spots' or areas where problems seem to be most serious, and to map together information about health, education, crime, service provision and so forth. Housing needs assessments, health audits and crime and disorder audits have all helped to identify local needs. In addition, a number of local authorities have begun to work with people within local areas to explore their needs, ideas and visions for the future.

Understanding customers

Consultation is a vital way of gathering management data in order to assess the success of service delivery. Regular public opinion surveys about the council as a whole can offer feedback about whether local people think you are 'doing a good job' and service-specific surveys can help to understand what people think about particular services. Combining qualitative and quantitative data can be very important, and using focus groups, mystery visitors, user consultants and other techniques will help to evaluate the quality of services.

In the private sector market analysis is seen as an integral part of research and development (R&D) – a vital area of investment for the future. However, public sector organizations often fail to invest in R&D; they spend virtually no time at all in designing and developing new series and products, or in market consultation and analysis. Compared to the private sector, local authorities know precious little about what their customers think of their products or why.

Over time, services become more and more outdated until they finally become obsolete, and it is vital to invest in the development of replacement services before the old ones have to be abandoned. Without far better customer understanding, such investment is impossible. We need to recognize, as the private sector does, the wide diversity of service users, and the different needs they have, for example to understand that the way a young working mum might use a housing service might be different from the way it would be used by an elderly pensioner. In addition, we need to recognize that young people want different advice services to older people and that leisure services that fit the needs of men will not necessarily be interesting or attractive to women. By 'segmenting' customers, and researching carefully the views and perspectives of different segments, we can begin to understand the diversity of different lifestyles and needs represented within our communities, and plan to meet them more effectively.

Helping to determine local priorities

Local authorities have a role as community leaders, and are increasingly taking responsibility for producing community plans, co-ordinating action from a range of agencies to tackle social problems. This role makes it more and more important to understand the ideas, aspirations and priorities of local people. In order to focus attention on the problems that matter most to local people, it is vital first to know what they are. Often professionals and politicians carry untested assumptions about what matters to local people, and can get bogged down in internal problems that are not important to the wider public.

Many local authorities are now beginning to involve and engage local people in thinking about the future of the locality itself. What should it be like? What do local people want the area to be like? What do they aspire to? What matters most to them? What do they need?

Innovating to solve social problems

Many of the complex problems that we face occur at the interface between different services. The public can be a valuable source of ideas – because people's lives are not separated out into different professional boxes – so members of the public often have a clearer and more holistic picture of how services are experienced than providers do. By engaging with people in the community in thinking about a particular problem, it can be possible to access new ideas, new ways of thinking 'outside the box' and find new ways of doing things. To do this, local councils need to engage with people in open dialogue, sharing information, analysis and decision-making. It often means finding new ways of working and 'virtual' arrangements outside the conventional local authority structures.

Innovation involves risk and local people can help to assess and to reduce the risks involved in new initiatives. They can also help to share the risk by agreeing to new experiments. Local people also have down-to-earth knowledge about how and why things go wrong. By using users or members of the public as discussants or consultants or by engaging them in the design of new services, it is possible to iron out design faults in advance.

Drawing in new resources – creating social capital

The most frequently heard complaint by local government managers is that they have not got enough resources to respond to local people's needs. This is often accompanied by fears that consultation will simply raise expectations, and lead to increasing demands for the scarce and shrinking supply of resources.

We suggest that community engagement should be considered the other way round, as a potential source of new resources to meet local needs. It is true that local government resources are finite, and there is little prospect of more money. It is, therefore, important to think about resources in new ways. Many of the problems that pubic managers are trying to tackle – poor school performance, vandalism on estates, overload of GPs – cannot be solved by professionals working alone. Solutions require the support and commitment of local people, and often need attitudes and behaviours to change. If members of the wider public are involved in identifying problems and working out ways to tackle them, they are more likely to support the course of action chosen, and to commit resources to it in the form of voluntary effort. The relationships built during consultation, the opportunities to talk to neighbours and fellow citizens, can help to strengthen local communities. Baby-sitting rotas and social activity sometimes follow.

In areas where unemployment is high and the sense of social exclusion is strong, local people may lack the energy or confidence to seek training or work, and may feel powerless and, therefore, apathetic about changing things. Professional behaviours have sometimes made things worse, by patronizing local people or by insisting on bureaucratic rules rather than building solutions that make sense locally. For years now, council staff have been developing new skills, capabilities and behaviours (although there is still a lot of work to be done to build up the skills of many mainstream staff). Many local managers and staff are now developing the skills across all service areas to work in partnership with all sections of the community, even those who have been most excluded, young unemployed people for example. Community engagement offers opportunities to build the skills, knowledge and capacity of local people.

CONCLUSION

Often, there is no single one of these 'drivers' for engaging the community operating in isolation. In reality, managers will be dealing with what happens when several of these drivers are operating at once, and when they collide in interesting ways.

This leads to a number of emerging dilemmas. These are not management 'problems' that have a simple or a single solution. These dilemmas are permanent, because they represent the tension between different pressures, and good managers have to find a way to create the right balance of response. That means understanding the complexity, and learning how to manage into it by building a simple and clear path on which to walk.

In later chapters we explore further some of the approaches available, the problems that will need to be tackled when implementing them, and some possible solutions. For local government managers at all levels, 'managing with the public' has become a core skill or capacity. At senior level, managers will need to design effective methods of consultation, plan feedback and lead the organizational change necessary to respond. Middle managers will be involved in discussion and planning of consultation, often taking initiatives at local level and working with community leaders, and rethinking services alongside local people. Front-line staff will be actively engaged in listening to and responding to local people's views and comments, and involved in planning and implementing change.

2 Choosing a method

Sue Goss

INTRODUCTION

There is no one simple way of engaging with the public. There are many techniques being developed; some creative, some practical, some brief and simple, others involving sustained dialogue. There is considerable knowledge and expertise inside local authorities, in the community and in other agencies. Nevertheless, the experience of different local authorities is very diverse, and while some managers are familiar with a range of methods, and able to develop new ones, others are struggling, and are familiar only with one or two approaches. In a survey of the consultation methods being used by local authorities in 1998, Figure 2.1 shows the most common consultation methods.

Of course, experience is developing fast, and many more authorities are developing expertise in approaches that were virtually unknown a few years ago. At the moment these can seem to be a bewildering variety. A number of helpful guides have been produced on this subject and these are listed in the 'Further reading' section at the end of this book. What has been missing in the past is a 'vocabulary' through which managers can sort out the different approaches to the public and make sense of the different methods and their strengths and weaknesses. Our views in this book are inevitably subjective, based on our experience and practice, but the intention in this chapter is to explore the different approaches and to set out a range of dimensions on which these differences can be analysed in order to help frame the right choice for the right situation.

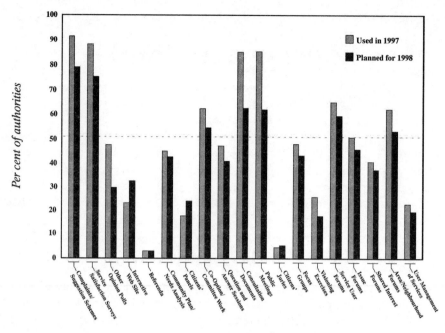

Form of participation

Source: DETR, 1998

Figure 2.1   Most common consultation methods

 Task

Look at the chart in Figure 2.1. Think about your own service. Which methods have you used and what were they used for?

Talk about this with some colleagues from other departments. List the different techniques that have been used and what they were used for.

Then make a list for the rest of the chapter of those that no one has used. Read the rest of this chapter being mindful of taking some information back to your colleagues about what is distinctive about these methods.

Choosing which method to use should not be seen as a 'technical problem' or as a problem simply for specialists. Indeed, we have some serious concerns about what might happen if mainstream managers saw public engagement as 'nothing to do with them' or an issue for experts. We know that there are many specialist market research companies, and consultancies offering important support and help, but many of them only offer a limited set of 'products' or do so from a particular perspective, or are specialized in only a very narrow range of areas. A research consultancy may not help you with the problem of getting councillors to hear and respond to very critical views. A consultancy with expertise in listening to tenants, or service users, may not be able to sort out the internal management problems you encounter when trying to respond. If you call in a market research company you will get market research. If you choose 'planning for real' then that is the technique that will be used. In reality, there is seldom a single technique or approach that will work, and often different approaches make sense at different points in time, or in different situations.

Local government managers need to develop a core competence in deciding what sort of approach makes sense locally, and in creating the right environment within which engagement will succeed. As we gain confidence and skill, we should be able to design and develop our own methods, and learn to combine approaches in ways that tackle the specific needs of our organizations and communities. To be able to make an informed choice about which method to use you need to know:

- about all the possible methods available;
- the nature of the task that you want to use the method for;
- the nature of the public that you are wanting to consult.

If you know all three of these you will be in a position to make an informed choice.

 Task

Think about the last time you or your department carried out a consultation. Were you able to fully answer the above three questions? If not, where were the main absences from the discussion? Did you know the full range of methods? Did you ensure that they were fit for the purpose of the consultation method? Do you know the specific characteristics of the public that you were trying to engage with?

A two-way process

However, any process of working with the public is (at least) two-way. It is plain daft to design an approach to engagement that does not take account of the views of people within the communities with which you want to engage. Some authorities have conducted formal consultations with people about how they want to be consulted; others have taken informal soundings or co-opted people from the relevant communities on to steering groups or project groups. Some have handed over the design and management of consultation processes to local people. However it is done, any process of consultation needs to learn from what is already known about user views, build on existing knowledge about mood and concerns, and what sorts of method have succeeded or failed in the past. Everyone is familiar with stories about the public meeting to discuss the performance plan that ran into public outrage about a hospital closure, the organized band of political activists that disrupted a consultation meeting, or the hostility created by consultation about regeneration on an estate where basic services were failing. Without careful planning, and good understanding between organizations and departments, and between the public and the council, time and energy can be wasted. At each stage in consultation – by the local authority or partners – knowledge is gained on all sides which can be used to design and plan what happens next. A bureaucratic, hermetically sealed plan is unlikely to achieve as much as a process of evolving shared dialogue, in which local people feel they can shape the process, as well as express their views.

Members of the public, or service users, are not simply able to play a role in information-gathering. They can also be actively engaged in delivery, service management, and planning and evaluation.

Local councils may be able to act as community leaders, or as the co-ordinators of a performance plan or community plan, but other people have resources that can help to make things happen. Making the best use of all the possible contributions is a powerful test of an enabling council. Given the importance of public consultation to all public organizations it is likely that every public sector organization in your locality is developing a consultation strategy with the public. It is almost certain that these will have been developed separately from each other and in many cases will contain duplication. The public will find it odd to be asked similar questions by different organizations. It is important to work across boundaries.

 Task

Do you know what the public consultation strategy is for the other public sector organizations in your area – the health service, police and educational institutions? It is important to start to gather that information.

DIFFERENT STAGES OF CONSULTATION

One of the best known descriptions of the different stages of consultation is Arnstein's ladder of participation (Arnstein, 1971), which suggests a series of stages beginning with manipulation, therapy and informing, progressing to consultation and placation, and then to partnership, delegated power and citizen control. The most usual criticism of the Arnstein 'ladder' is that it implies that ascending the ladder is always right and that the 'higher' stages of participation are preferable to the 'lower' stages. In reality, the right approach depends on the preferences and choice of local people, as well as what is practicable.

These distinctions have been helpfully reworked by Burns *et al* in the 1980s, to reflect three types of participation:

- 'citizen non-participation' (provision of information);
- 'citizen participation' (consultation);
- 'citizen control' (involving citizen control over budget setting and policy).

One possible 'community engagement spectrum' involves four stages as shown in Figure 2.2:

Information provision ⟶ Consultation ⟶ Involvement ⟶ Delegation

Source: DETR, 1999

Figure 2.2   Different stages of consultation

The problem is that this sort of model easily leads to an approach that is very centred on the local authority and what it does, rather than seeing the wider range of relationships and ways of doing things that become available once we break out of narrow organizational boundaries. We need additional 'headings' to reflect the wider range of approaches that involve visioning, innovating and planning action collaboratively. If we adapt this model slightly, we can see in Table 2.1 that a number of different approaches map reasonably comfortably on to the sorts of reason for engaging with the public that we explored in the last chapter.

Table 2.1 Reasons for engaging with the public

Enlightened self-interest	Understanding communities	Innovating	Setting priorities	Social capital building
Information provision	Consulting/ listening	Exploring/ innovating/ visioning	Judging/ deciding together	Delegating/ supporting decision making

In practice, however, as the Warwick team point out 'the boundaries between the different approaches to engagement, and the specific approaches may well fall into more than one category'. (DETR, 1999). Frameworks like this are useful to build understanding, but do not offer sufficient specificity to select a particular method or approach.

Table 2.2 attempts to group loosely the current range of methods for engagement and the different categories. Each method is explored in brief at the end of this chapter, but several are explored in greater depth in later chapters.

Table 2.2 Current range of methods for engagement

Giving Information	Consultation/ Listening	Exploring/ Innovating/ Visioning	Judging/ Deciding Together	Delegating/ Supporting/ Decision-making
sign-posting	surveys	consultative workshops	deliberative polls	neighbourhood committees
leaflets/ newsletters/ reports	focus groups	Visioning workshops	citizens' juries	town/estate plans
	priority search			
community profiles	interactive community profiles	simulations, open-space events	negotiation workshops	tenant management organizations
feedback on surveys and consultation	public meetings forums		community issue groups	
annual performance reports			community workshops	Community development, trust
support/advice	panels	planning for real community discovery	consensus conferences	partnerships/ contracts with communities
video/Internet communication	video boxes	use of theatre, arts/media		referendums/ tele-voting

There are other factors which need to be taken into account, such as geographical boundaries, the size of the population to be consulted, the different sorts of legitimacy required, the different stages over time, the level of creativity and innovation required, and the skills, resources and readiness of the authority itself. In the following section, we attempt to set out the different dimensions which will influence choice.

LEGITIMACY AND DIVERSITY

There are a range of different interests held within a community, and it is important to be able to understand and hear from every section of the community, without becoming confused about the different interests being expressed.

The first stages of community involvement often involve working with local voluntary organizations which have a wider network of contacts within the community, and can represent specific interests, such as the elderly, or people with disabilities. However, sometimes that is as far as it goes, and organizations are asked to 'speak for' local people without an understanding that these organizations often also have interests as providers of services, or vested interests in certain theories or approaches, or as campaigning or lobby groups. It is important to be clear about the 'legitimacy' that organizations and individuals carry.

As members of the public we have a range of very different interests in what the council does. We are not all customers of all council services. We may find that we have conflicting interests – even as an individual. At one and the same time the individual might be a parent, a school governor, a library service user, a local resident, a car owner, a tax payer, a member of an ethnic minority, a woman, a member of council staff, a local volunteer and the chair of a local tenants' association.

In each of these roles we have more or less information about council activities, and more or less 'legitimacy' when we express an opinion. By legitimacy we mean an acknowledged 'right' to be consulted on an issue or a sense that one's view has particular validity. Legitimacy can come from a number of sources, it can come from being particularly knowledgeable, being a professional for example. It can come from 'representing' a large number of other people. It can come from having had a powerful experience, for example of a chronic illness, which has built understanding.

We need to understand and take account of these different sorts of 'legitimacy' in order to understand whose views we need to take into account, and what are the best methods of engagement. It is not a matter of deciding that some sorts of legitimacy are better than others. Elected representatives of a tenants' association, for example carry considerable weight, but their views are not always representative of all sections of the community. On the other hand, simply asking a random selection of six women about what women wanted in the borough would give valuable information, but it would not carry the same weight. In reality, we need to learn from people with all these sorts of legitimacy; to learn from expertise, opinion, experience, knowledge and organized interest groups.

However, we need to be very clear why we are asking people to be involved, and what sort of role we are asking them to play. If we are asking them to speak for others, there may be a need for them to go themselves and consult and check out views, or to get feedback from a wider group about their contribution. If we are asking people to speak from their own experiences, they may need opportunities to think and talk through them in order to reach a point of view. If we are asking people to 'be themselves', but to take part in a citizen's jury or panel, then we need to create opportunities for people to reflect on their own legitimacy, and to engage in discussion about the right ways to use their views and knowledge. In several citizens' juries, jury members have felt perfectly happy that elected representatives make a final decision and do not simply act on their recommendations, but have wanted to make sure that their hard work was recognized and sufficient weight given to their careful deliberations.

Thinking about how to reach people

One of the most depressing complaints is that people do not want to be involved. It is often said that this is because of the failure of a series of public meetings, an empty room at an estate consultation meeting or a low response rate to a postal questionnaire, or a tiny response rate to an advertisement in the local council newspaper. The question is why would people want to be involved? What's in it for them? Why might it be in their interests? We know that people turn up when they are very angry. If we fail sufficiently seriously, we can motivate people to override the other priorities in their life and come and tell us about it. The interesting question is whether or not we can find ways to motivate people when they are not angry. Anecdotal evidence suggests that the public are quite good at 'reading' the motivation and seriousness of a local authority which tries to involve them. A vague, poorly planned process, which looks boring and which may not lead to action, will get a poor response. A well-focused, well-organized process, where it is clear why it is happening and what will happen next, will do better. Best of all are those processes where prospective participants have had a chance to decide what they might want to get out of it, and how they want to take part, and the authority has made a prior commitment to act on the learning that emerges.

30

Much depends on the level of commitment we are asking from people. If it is a substantial commitment – to a focus group, panel, workshop, visioning event and so forth – we need to offer quite a high level of commitment to the participants. This means not simply making the process exciting, entertaining, giving people an opportunity to do things they would like to do, but paying attention to high levels of feedback about progress, and making a commitment to act on the learning that comes from the process. If we are simply gathering data, we need to make the process relatively unobtrusive, not time-consuming or difficult, and to be able to explain why it is helpful, and how they as citizens might benefit. More time and attention needs to be focused on winning the interest of the public, and understanding why, and when, they want to get involved.

Different audiences can be reached in different ways. The first step is to identify the different 'communities' or sections of the community that live in a locality, and think about how best to understand their needs and concerns. This can be done through brainstorming, stakeholder mapping, workshops with service users themselves and consultation about how people want to be consulted. The important thing is to plan public engagement based on an understanding of what the public may want to talk about. If different sections of the community have different interests, or are likely to be willing to take part in different processes, we may want to segment our audience carefully. By thinking about the needs and choices of the audience, rather than by doing things in old ways, many local authorities have begun a dialogue with groups of people that have in the past been unimpressed by local government and seen it as irrelevant to their lives. It is not difficult to work alongside people for whom English is not a first language, or young businesspeople, or teenagers. However, we have to do it in ways that make sense to them, not simply through committee meetings and reports.

Case study: Tower Hamlets

Tower Hamlets Council's development of a vision for the area targeted a number of 'hard to reach' population groups (youth, Bengali women who do not speak English, and people with disabilities). Community 'guides' were recruited and trained, to recruit a representative cross-section of each population group, and help with the facilitation of a series of community workshops. This process created a trustworthy link between the community and the engagement process, developed new community skills and involved members of the community who, in the past, had not been included in public consultation.

If we are trying to engage young people, we can develop techniques that will work with and for them. We have young creative staff scattered across the local authority and we have links with schools, local colleges and youth clubs; we often fund media, theatre or other projects. Many authorities have been successful in engaging with young people in new and exciting ways.

Case study: Birmingham City Council

Birmingham City Council targeted young people and held a series of meetings in 1996 to which they attracted over 500 young people aged between 13 and 21. Meetings included targeted meetings for young women, and disabled young people. The feedback processes were designed with young people in mind, and included 'graffiti walls' and response sheets.

Case study: Homelessness charities

A number of homelessness charities dealing with young street homeless people have discovered that they are unwilling to take part in meetings or to talk much to professional staff in formal settings about their views. However, the installation of interactive computer programmes in day centres or hostels has enabled young people to choose a moment when they feel able and willing to comment on their views and experience, and to do so without having to face a professional interviewer with whom they may feel uncomfortable or embarrassed about their situation.

Representing diversity

Once we have recognized the diversity and breadth of interests within the community, we can ensure that whatever methods we use, this diversity is represented. It is possible to balance the recruitment of interviewees, panel members, focus group members and citizen juries to reflect the balance in the wider community. Rather than a random sample, these are usually based on a 'balanced sample', in which the random recruitment is done to ensure the right proportions of participants from different sections of the community. This cannot be done easily in very small samples, and the number of variables that can sensibly be chosen is limited. It will be possible to ensure that samples reflect gender, ethnicity, age and so forth; it would be harder (though not impossible) to get a balance of sports fans, library users and *Sun* readers.

It may be helpful, rather than simply balancing representation in workshops and focus groups, to bring together people with a common experience or interest – to hold focus groups of older people or young people. An interesting second stage can be to bring together the different groups to explore their differences and similarities, and begin a process of real life exploration of common ground and possible ways forward.

Understanding obstacles to participation

Whatever process we choose, we know there are significant obstacles which have tended to exclude some people from full citizenship in the past. We need to bear these in mind, and ensure that we can hear those voices that have traditionally gone unheard. These may be those of people who have faced discrimination – women, the ethnic minority communities and people with physical disabilities. They may be those of people whose lives are most unlike those of councillors and senior managers, for example teenagers and young mums at home. They may be those of people who do not play a role in civic affairs, transient populations and people who work long hours. They may be those of people who do not have the confidence to speak at public meetings, or who are not literate in English, or who have mental health problems.

 Task

Next time you are in a meeting with senior managers in your council, look around the room at the age gender ethnicity and clothing of the people in the room. Note the proportion of people from different sections and how they look and talk. Sometime later that week go to the local shopping centre or market nearest to your office. Spend a few minutes looking at the people shopping there. Look at their age, ethnicity, gender and clothing. Chart the differences between these two groups.

If group 1 wants to consult, group 2 think through the problems they may have.

There is a strong literature now about ways to include disadvantaged sections of the community in consultation processes. There is also considerable knowledge about good ways to ensure that engaging the public is an inclusive process, and these are explored in Chapter 8. There is not sufficient space in this book to repeat all the lessons that have been learnt from practice, but a good starting point would be the books set out in the 'Further reading' section at the end of this book. A good knowledge of the issues and practical solutions are important starting points for any manager who will be designing or planning consultation.

Basics, such as ensuring that we communicate to communities who do not readily speak English, that we make access easy, that we provide support so that we do not exhaust or cause harm to groups or individuals who take time to help us, that we give people enough time to participate adequately, that we pay attention to their comfort, that processes are transparent and honest – all these have to be taken into account.

Often, time and resources do not make it possible to carry out a comprehensive process and short cuts have to be made. It may not be sensible to spend a fortune translating long and complicated documents into lots of languages, for example, especially since consultation around draft plans may be the wrong stage or the wrong process! There may be easier and more imaginative ways to involve different sections of the community. Trade-offs will be inevitable, but it is important to work with people from minority groups to explain and discuss the problems, and try to reach shared and sensible solutions that do not simply involve reverting to consultation approaches that may unintentionally exclude them. The questions, as always, will be: Why are we doing this? What do we hope to achieve? What is the best way to achieve this? How can we do that within the resources we have?

Private companies, other public bodies, community groups

Part of the audience of any consultation process will be other agencies. We need to recognize the differences between them, and not try to treat them all in the same way. For example, other public agencies will probably be relatively well focused on the public policy issues in the area, and predisposed to take part. They will be used to public consultation processes, and familiar with the procedural rules and traditional public sector constraints.

Private sector companies, and businesspeople on the other hand, may not be focused on the same problems and issues, and may not see the relevance to them of the work that we do. We often underestimate the level of interest private sector businesses have in the success of the local area and the quality of the local environment, but fail to capitalize on that interest. If they are to be involved in wider processes of consultation, they will need to see the relevance of what we are doing to them and to their interests. In the private sector, as the cliché goes, time is money, and managers and executives that take part in any process will often want to be clear that action will follow. They can become frustrated by bureaucracy, and want to ensure that responses will be rapid enough to justify their participation. On the other hand, they may be able to contribute resources and help in a far wider range of situations than we have traditionally considered.

Voluntary organizations are as diverse as the people they represent. Some are geared up to respond to local authority consultation, and are highly focused on local government policy. Some very local groups, at the other extreme, find it hard to communicate, have very few resources, and find it very hard to divert them towards wider consultation processes without weakening the group itself. In the early stages of consultation, it is easy to confuse voluntary organizations with the public and to assume that consultation is sufficient if voluntary or community groups have been involved. The reality is, of course, that voluntary organizations have their own interests and priorities, and while some do represent the diversity within a community others are representative of only one vociferous section. Some may be powerful service providers in their own right, and have business, as well as community, interests to represent.

Recognizing the different roles played by different voluntary groups and their strengths and weaknesses is an important part of planning any consultation process. It will be important to be clear when people from community groups or voluntary organizations are seen as 'representative' and when their legitimacy comes from personal knowledge and ideas.

FROM OPINION TO JUDGEMENT

Different techniques enable us to learn different things. In this section we suggest that it is important to determine whether or not we want to gather opinions, create new thinking or engage others in the process of reaching judgements.

Gathering opinions

A number of techniques such as surveys, interviews and focus groups enable us to identify *opinions*. These are our initial responses, with little thought or reflection, and often with only partial information.

Opinions can be very helpful, particularly if we are wanting to find out what the current state of thinking is about an issue. Opinion polls are vital to politicians because people will vote based on those opinions. Finding out how people view the area in which they live, whether they like the area, plan to stay, value the amenities, can help to plan regeneration policies. It is *opinions* we receive if we ask basic survey questions about satisfaction with different dimensions of local services.

Opinions are, therefore, relatively useful in helping us to establish a baseline; to help us gauge the level of support a particular action might have; to understand the way that public opinion is going, or to understand the facts that motivate people's choices or actions. However, as Robin Clarke points out in Chapter 4, opinions can be ill-informed, or arrived at without thought. Professionals are often concerned that we will fail to do the right thing if we act according to opinion, because the public do not properly understand the issues and problems. Of course, from our perspective as citizens, we may believe that professionals do not listen, and carry their own prejudices. On both sides there may be opinions that can be tested, challenged and changed.

 Task

Think about your own experience as a consumer of services rather than as a local government manager. How do you know about the services you consume and how they are produced? What would it feel like if, when next you bought clothes, someone was to ask you about the different machines that may be used in producing those clothes? How could you frame that interaction to make more sense of it?

Active thinking – changing our minds

When we change our minds we precisely change our own internal belief systems, based on a process of reasoning, deliberation, investigation and exploration. Most of us do not change our minds without reasons. If we are to venture beyond our current opinions, to think differently or to think again about an issue, we may need new information, or new ideas. We may need to test our ideas against those of others, and to explore differences. We may need an opportunity to build new options or solutions that we had not thought of before. An important part of any process of engagement is the space and time to engage people in creative thinking. The more innovative you want people to be, the more carefully the space has to be designed to engender creativity. We will not get creative thinking in conventional settings.

Forming judgements – making decisions

In some circumstances, we do not simply want to gather opinion, or to engage with the public in a process of exploration and innovation, but we want to develop a process that will help to form judgements that can guide future action. A judgement is a relatively stable view, taken after considerable reflection and deliberation, taking into account all the relevant factors and balancing the different and often competing outcomes that we are trying to achieve. A judgement should carry a weight that an opinion does not, and enables us to make decisions about action that should follow.

A citizens' jury or a deliberative poll creates space within the methodology to enable the participants to reach a judgement. It is important, however, to be clear about what happens to that judgement. How does it become a decision?

Traditionally, we have relied on the processes of deliberation that form part of the conventional managerial and political processes to reach decisions about the way forward for an area. There are a number of ways, however, in which partners from other agencies, or from community groups, or individuals within the community can be involved in a process of decision-making based on judgement. This could involve a process of devolved decision-making to neighbourhoods or localities, a process of contracting, through the mutual agreement of a community or estate plan, or a process of negotiation and consensus-building between different sections of the community.

Developing a process over time

In reality, the process of consultation may have a series of different stages, each designed to achieve a different objective. There may be a 'baseline' stage in which we find out about current opinion to map our starting point and plan future action. This is the stage in which gaining information and simply listening is the most important, and where legitimacy is less important than the breadth of voices heard. In this stage it matters a lot that we do not simply hear from organized groups, and are able to ensure that voices are not 'left out' of the process.

Then, there may be a stage of exploration or dialogue in which it is possible to explore at a deeper level the experiences and perceptions we have heard about, to engage local people in dialogue, to think creatively and to begin to form ideas about ways forward. Here we may be drawing on techniques that encourage exploration and creativity. Legitimacy will be drawn from experience and from the process of deliberation, and it will be important that those who take part are drawn from the different perspectives and interests, but they may not be expected to 'speak for' or to 'represent' others.

The third stage is about consensus-building, using the information and ideas generated to lead to decisions about a course of action. It is here that issues of legitimacy matter most. In some circumstances this is the stage in which elected councillors will want to ensure that they take the final decision, drawing on their legitimacy as elected representatives. In other circumstances – for example where the consent or support of other agencies or community groups will be essential if the plan is to succeed – there are other techniques that can be used, such as consensus conferences, open negotiations, multi-partner consensual contracts and so forth. In some cases, particularly, for example where special funding from the lottery or to fund regeneration work requires community agreement and action, there may be a neighbourhood-based process to develop final agreement to the plan. In any case it will be important to make sure that organizations and individuals whose resources, commitment and energy are necessary to make action work have been part of the decision-making process, and that those involved are sufficiently senior, or carry sufficient legitimacy and authority to speak on behalf of those they represent.

Geography and size

Geography plays a part in choosing methods. At a very basic level, dense urban communities can be involved in different ways to sparse rural communities. Places where there is considerable homogeneity, or close community ties, will make it possible to work in ways that make no sense if there are very diverse lifestyles and different communities of interest. Places where parish councils already exist may be able to use them, whereas in busy cities and towns there may be little sense of belonging to a locality. The number of people to be consulted is also important, and the size of the geographical space in which people live. A city or region requires different approaches to a ward or an estate.

READINESS AND CAPABILITY

It is important to think about the readiness and capability of the organization.

Resources and budgets

It is vital to match the approach chosen to the capability of the organization, and to the resources available. Different methods require very different levels of resources. A full-scale deliberative poll can cost £250,000 while focus groups or visioning events can cost only a few thousand pounds. The truth is, however, that there are very few 'cost-free' options, and all approaches carry an opportunity cost for the managers, staff and citizens who take part. Consultation processes should be seen as a very important investment in future service development and in planning future action, and treated with great seriousness. That does not mean that they should necessarily be expensive but they must maximize the value gained from the investment.

Organizational readiness

More significant than the planning of consultation itself is an assessment of the readiness of the organization to respond. Chapter 10 explores this further. It may be helpful to carry out a simple audit of organizational readiness, which will help you to identify the sorts of problem that you can expect. If you have any concerns about the capability of the council to respond rapidly and effectively, warning bells should sound. If the local authority has serious performance and communication problems they are bound to impact on the effectiveness of the consultation. If managers and staff already feel they are overworked and unable to cope, consultation will simply throw up more things they cannot cope with. If you anticipate difficulties inside the organization, it may help to start with a very small process that is highly targeted and from which results can be seen very fast, and to build up slowly to larger-scale exercises.

 Task

Involve a group of fellow managers in a rough and ready audit of the organization's readiness to respond to the consultation process you are carrying out. Identify the obstacles to change that you may encounter. How will you remove these obstacles?

Project planning

Good project planning is essential. It is important to think in advance about communication with staff and partners, the time-scales for further action and implementation, and the skills that may be needed.

It is also important to plan the level of resources that you need to match your objectives. This is not simply a matter of budgeting for a consultation process. It means planning the deployment of the managerial and staff time necessary to make the process a success, the contribution of elected members, and partners or colleagues within the community.

Good project planning means careful attention to detail by ensuring that members of the public experience a pleasant and convenient consultation, for example good information, friendly faces, good food, comfortable venues, hot coffee, maps and so forth. It means ensuring that any written materials have good design, graphics, plain English and so forth; that meetings are facilitated and chaired well and that processes are transparent and honest. Most of the problems that arise in consultation can be avoided if project planning is more effective in the early stages.

Experience tells us that two elements vital to success are often 'left out' of consultation processes; these are feedback and shared learning.

Feedback

Unless the people who take part can see for themselves the impact that their contribution has made, interest in consultation will begin to decay. Consultation fatigue is not caused by too much consultation, but by too little action. For many people the motivation for taking part is altruistic. Service users say things like: 'I want to make sure that what happened to me does not happen to anyone else'. Not only do we have to change things, we must then tell people about what we have changed, perhaps involving them in the next step. Engagement can be cumulative, with people taking a greater interest and role as they learn more. Processes of engagement are about building a two-way relationship and this is built in a number of stages. As individuals, we make judgements about the seriousness with which we are treated, and make decisions to invest our own time and energy in response. Without feedback about progress, the experience of participants is sterile. As much energy needs to be invested in feedback to each individual who takes part, through a report, a newsletter, a leaflet, a telephone call or a follow-up discussion, as in the process of consultation itself.

Creating a learning process

Any process of consultation or engagement offers opportunities for learning throughout the organization – most directly to those involved, but also to colleagues, other councillors and senior managers, front-line staff, ordinary members of the community who take part and partner agencies. If techniques are exploratory or new, then the potential for learning must be exploited; to learn how things could be done better in the future, and to help colleagues in other departments learn the lessons from the experiment. Complex processes of engagement are unlikely to be 'right first time' and unless we apply a robust degree of scepticism and challenge, we are unlikely to achieve 'best value' in consultation. Local government managers need to find ways to make experimentation safe, and fun, while keeping the learning and the resulting analysis sharp.

'BRINGING THE PUBLIC INTO THE MAINSTREAM'

Public engagement does not always require a specially commissioned process or event. There are a number of ways that public views and experiences can be built into the mainstream delivery of local services. At the most basic, complaints or 'job done' user satisfaction cards can be used as the basis for regular debriefing and rethinking services. User feedback can be fed into day-to-day planning through the analysis of the choices users make, for example choices of meals, volume of use of different leisure facilities, levels of usage at different times of the day and so forth. Many services have integrated user panels or steering groups into day-to-day services, for example the Bexley Council 'park users group' or user steering groups in leisure centres. In many residential care homes users form residents' committees to advise about day-to-day issues. Social services business units often have focus groups or user forums for each client group, such as people with disabilities, or people with learning difficulties. These groups contribute to thinking on care management and future service development.

In housing it is usual to have tenants' associations, tenants' federations, tenant forums, neighbourhood committees, tenant representatives on housing committees and so forth, although historically there is less experience of the consultation of leaseholders, private tenants, landlords and owner-occupiers. Some of the most advanced models for transferring control over services to users occur in housing, where there is considerable experience of co-operatives, tenant management organizations, community-based housing associations, local housing companies, estate management boards and so forth. In social services there have been experiments in user-run services. Much of this experience could be translated to other services.

On an authority-wide basis there are experiments in devolved management, including area committees, neighbourhood committees and neighbourhood partnerships. Increasingly, these experiments in devolution involve other public agencies as well as the local council, involve the private sector as well as the public sector and involve access to substantial funding.

An integrated consultation strategy

Perhaps the most important questions to ask when designing a consultation strategy are: 'Does it fit well with corporate goals?' 'Will doing this help to achieve the changes we want to see as a council?' 'Does it cut across or duplicate the work of others?' 'Does it help to focus energy and attention on the things that matter?'

The design of any process of public engagement, therefore, has to take account of what else is going on across the authority and with partners' organizations and ensure that the approach chosen makes sense in the context of the wider demands on the authority. Managing with the public must be integrated with other work on performance plans or community plans, best value, experimental action zones and local priorities such as regeneration.

Conclusion: choosing the right method

The right method for managing working with the public emerges through a discussion which involves a consideration of all the following elements:

- the reasons for engagement;
- the stages of consultation chosen (giving information/listening/vision-ing/acting together/supporting devolved decision-making);
- the balance required between opinion and judgement;
- the length of process envisaged – one single approach or a combination;
- the role people are being asked to take (as representatives, as individuals);
- the nature of the audience/audiences;
- the best ways to reach excluded sections of the community;
- the geography/size of the population to be engaged;
- the process in which you are wanting engagement (getting ideas, planning services, taking action, evaluation);
- the resources available;
- the readiness of the authority to respond;
- the best way to give feedback to participants;
- the best way to ensure that others learn from the process;
- the best way to create an integrated process that meets wider council goals.

 Task

In Chapter 1 we asked you to start collecting all the different examples of public consultation that you could from your local authority. We agreed that this was a massive task – in itself proving the issue about a lack of co-ordination. Read them through again in the light of this section about strategy and start to think what a strategy would look like that brought all these together.

BRIEF GUIDE TO DIFFERENT METHODS FOR MANAGING WORKING WITH THE PUBLIC

In the following section we set out some of the main techniques currently in use, which can be combined together into an overall approach to match local needs. Further methods can be found in the books in the 'Further reading' section, particularly those by Stewart (1995, 1996).

Giving information

Giving good, understandable information is a basic first step for any consultation process. Newsletters, local council papers and leaflets are an important part of general communication. Many local authorities now check their information, leaflets, brochures, Web site and so forth with user consultants or focus groups to make sure it is easy to understand. Feedback on the quality of your information is essential. There is plenty of guidance about how to use plain English, and how to communicate well with people who have visual or auditory disabilities, or people for whom English is not their first language. Careful attention is needed not only to the wording, but to the design, layout and ways of ensuring that people can access information. Signposting and communication between departments is as important as good communication within a department. Some authorities provide handbooks or brochures about local services, computer access points at town halls or libraries, or Web Sites. Some include 'chat-lines', and feedback systems. Using wider media – local radio, TV, community media systems – is also helpful.

Performance reports

Councils are now expected to report to local people about their performance against the targets and goals they have set themselves; more attention is being paid to making these eye-catching and interesting. Lewisham, for example, produces a highly designed 'Annual Report' which reports on progress in the previous year, with strong use of colour, graphics and quotes from local people.

Training the public

Some authorities have begun to offer training to local people to enable them to take part more effectively. An experiment in consultation led by the Portsmouth Health Authority involved the local technical college providing a training course on the National Health Service to help members of the public learn about how the service works. Experiments have included the use of NVQ level one qualifications to train service users to be able to take part in service planning discussions. There are opportunities for joint training, linking voluntary organizations and community groups into mainstream training programmes within the authority. Many schools now provide citizenship education, and authorities such as Leicester provide teaching resource packs that explain how European, national and local government works, and gives information about their city and County Council.

Open days and exhibitions

Many authorities have experimented with new ways to communicate to the public, and have established open days, exhibitions in libraries, shopping centres and so forth and interactive exhibitions. Thurrock, for example, set up an exhibition in the main shopping centre, which spelt out several different possible solutions for a community scheme, and asked members of the public, once they had read the different alternatives, to register a preference, giving their reasons.

Electronic communication

Increasingly, local authorities use the Internet to communicate with local populations. Lewisham and Brent provide details of committee meetings. Hampshire put minutes on the Internet. At present, of course, this is problematic as only a very small proportion of the public have access to the Internet. Over time, this may become a far more important form of communication. Norwich is proposing to link communication together and to provide access to the Internet in libraries and so forth.

Listening/researching/gathering feedback

Complaint and feedback systems

Councils are increasingly investing in good complaints and feedback systems. This can include comments cards at the point of service delivery, or 'job done' cards for work carried out on people's homes to ensure that it has been done to their satisfaction. Many private companies regularly send out 'post-service' surveys, with rewards such as prize draws for filling them in. A captive audience, for example in a waiting room, will often take the time to fill in forms about their experience of the service. It is important to encourage complaints and feedback as they provide vital management information and to make it easy and pleasant to complain! That will mean not necessarily assuming that more complaints means service failure. Work to understand why complaints happen and to track the patterns of complaints is also important. Similarly, comment systems have to ensure that service users and staff get regular feedback about the comments that have been made, and the action taken.

Community profiles

Community profiles offer useful starting points for any consultation process. They involve gathering information about the local community, and creating a database that can form the basis for consultation. Information could include census data, information about the groups that make up the community, on age, relative wealth or deprivation, family size, health, employment, crime and so forth, and can help to pinpoint concentrations of groups it is traditionally difficult to reach, or areas on which to concentrate attention. They can also help to monitor the effectiveness of the action the council and partners take to tackle the problems identified. Some organizations draw on predictions from national bodies such as the Organization for Economic Co-operation and Development (OECD), the Local Government Management Board (LGMB) or the Henley Centre for Forecasting, or use consultants to draw up these profiles, which can then form the basis for scenario planning, or exercises to test out different possible future scenarios.

Public meetings

Public meetings are perhaps the most familiar method of consultation. They are included under listening/researching/feedback, since they are seldom decision-making, or organized in ways that enable learning to take place. Their main function seems to be to gauge vocal public reaction to important proposals, and to allow a space for 'letting off steam' in a relatively formal process. Public meetings can be positive and consensual, but too often they have been organized in the past in ways which accentuate hierarchical relationships and encourage an adversarial exchange. To get the best use out of public meetings, it helps to plan the process carefully, breaking people up into discussion groups, organizing 'question time' sessions or enabling people to explore ideas and alternatives, rather than simply having a platform of speakers with questions at the end.

Surveys

Chapter 3 sets out some of the important design issues in relation to surveys in more depth. They can be either quantitative (a wide representative sample offering the possibility of quantifiable data in the form of x per cent of respondents believe you) or qualitative in-depth interviews which offer a richer information on why people hold the views they do, but does not offer the breadth of coverage that would enable qualifiable conclusions to be drawn. Surveys can be designed to elicit opinions on the local area, on current public services, on views of the council's performance in areas where people have experience, on people's expectations of their own future and on their own plans. However, they are not appropriate for exploring issues where people need considerable information in order to express a view. In-depth qualitative interviews can be used in relatively small numbers to improve the diagnostic power of wider surveys and to understand issues in depth. They can also be useful in understanding in detail personal experiences that individuals have had of services, and are particularly helpful in exploring the views of those who are not able or willing to take part in meetings, to fill in gaps or to explore in depth the perspective of very influential stakeholders.

User panels

There are a wide range of examples of user panels; forums or groups of users brought together on a relatively informal basis to discuss issues of service management or service development, or to act as a sounding board for new ideas. Many of these have been set up in the field of social services as a result of the encouragement to user consultation within community care arrangements, and forums have been established around client groups such as the elderly, or carers, or around particular services. They tend to be very focused on council service provision and are usually only advisory.

Focus groups

Focus groups are small-group discussions of around eight to ten people, and are led by a trained facilitator in a structured but open-ended discussion of a particular topic. The groups may be selected using a sampling process such as those used in surveys, or they can be organized according to particular interests such as the users of a particular service, or young people. It is often more useful to understand in depth the different perspectives of different groups and then to undertake a process that brings these different sets of views together. A discussion guide is usually put together by the commissioners of the focus groups, and the facilitator helps the group though a discussion of these issues. There are a number of basic rules of thumb to ensure that the group works well, and in addition to the skill of the facilitator, successful focus groups require careful choice of the venue, the level of support offered, the recruitment process, feedback and so forth.

Mystery shoppers/mystery visitors

These are processes used frequently within the private sector which enable managers and staff to find out about the consumers' experience of the services they offer. A 'mystery shopper', a specially briefed member of staff, a consultant or a 'user consultant' – a real service user who is paid to act as a consultant for the exercise – experiences an element of the service, and then reports back to managers and staff. User consultants can be particularly valuable when the service is targeted on a section of the population who are not well represented among senior managers and staff, for example people with physical disabilities, teenage mothers or the young unemployed. It is in any case helpful to ensure that the mystery shopper is not too well informed about the service, and is able to provide a different perspective, but will need to have the skills to observe and report back accurately.

Citizens' panels

Panels are a standing group of citizens who are regularly surveyed. Panels are usually made up of 1,000 participants or more and enable a good statistical sample to be made on a range of issues (see Chapter 3 for more information.) The larger the size of the panel, the more significant the views of any sub-groups identified within the panel (ie older people, women, owner-occupiers etc). They are surveyed either by telephone or in person, and panels can be used for a range of different purposes. The government has established its own citizens' panel, which it consults regularly. Panels can be used as the basis for a much wider range of consultation approaches:

Case study: Lewisham panel

In Lewisham, we have worked with the council to set up a Citizens' Panel. The 1,000-strong panel is surveyed by telephone and panel members are also asked to participate in focus groups and community conferences. People are panel members for a maximum of three years, during which time they build up considerable knowledge of the council and local issues. This is one of the ways that Lewisham is building active citizenship in the borough.

Panels 'decay' over time as people drop out, or move from the area, and need to be renewed from time to time. Bradford replace a third of their panel each year.

Case study: Bradford 'speak out'

Bradford Metropolitan Council, the Bradford Community Health NHS Trust and the Bradford and District TEC have jointly established a panel of 2,500 local residents, representative of the community in terms of employment, area where they live, age, gender and so forth. See Bradford Metropolitan Borough Council pack on Research Panels, obtainable from the research section.

Interactive technology

A number of authorities have been experimenting with the use of new technology, such as video-boxes (Newport), video-conferencing (Newham), Internet information lines (Cheshire). As we suggest in Chapter 7, the use of direct electronic voting is now possible, but has not been used. Over time, as Internet use becomes more common, the use of electronic referendums may become more popular. Interactive technology, including the use of computer handsets, can be used in visioning or consultation events to gain instant feedback about the views of a large group of people, and to track how views change during an event.

Priority search

Priority search is a methodology developed and owned by Priority Search Ltd, a British company founded in 1987. It is basically a survey technique, but by using an effective paired comparison technique it allows respondents to prioritize their responses. Specialized numerical techniques are used to produce relatively rich management information about the preferences and choices of service users.

The technique requires relatively large sample sizes, and is dependent on the use of the software and techniques that are only available through the Priority Search company, although they will license software to other end users.

Exploring/innovating/visioning

Community self-auditing

Community auditing is one term that is used for processes that involve the community in building up a picture of their local community. It may involve local people in meetings, workshops or 'strengths, weaknesses, opportunities, threats' (SWOT) analyses, to share views about the area as a prelude to agreeing shared action. Similar exercises have been called 'village appraisals' in South Somerset, where the village takes part in a village design day to explore the community's needs and the things that make it special. The LGMB (1997) guide, *Involving the Public* quotes examples from South Somerset District Council and North Kesteven District Council.

Community visioning

Visioning can involve a wide range of processes – it can be done using fliers or leaflets inviting people to list three wishes or help build a vision – or facilitated workshops can be used to share ideas about the present and the future, brainstorm possibilities and set priorities. Trained facilitators can lead groups of participants through guided visualization or inspirited envisioning – through a mental journey. 'Imagine' is a term coined in the USA to include ongoing processes of visioning within a loose framework, often including different groups within a community, for example children and older people (see Chapter 6 for more information).

Community discovery

Community discovery can be used to enable large groups of local people to focus not on current services, but on desired outcomes, and enables them to develop their own ideas about the sorts of service they would like to see and the linkages needed between them. The technique was launched in the London Borough of Lewisham and is described in a recent report by the Public Management Foundation (1998) (see Chapter 6).

Search events/future search/search conferences

These draw upon the 'future search technique' created by Marvin Weisbord and the 'search conference' devised by Merelyn Emery and bring together a number of elements of consultation and visioning into a three-day self-managed conference for key stakeholders in the community. The conference goes through a process of reviewing the past, exploring the present, creating possible desirable futures, trying to identify common ground between participants and agreeing action plans (see Chapter 6).

Planning for real

'Planning for real' is a well-known approach to involving communities in developing ideas about a geographical area. Using a three-dimensional model of the area, people attach their ideas, comments and reactions using flags or objects – the map evolves over a few weeks and can involve wide participation.

Use of theatre/media

A number of authorities have begun to use improvization, theatre and visual techniques to make participation more immediate, and more meaningful. Act Create Experience (ACE) and Participatory Theatre are examples of this. Some authorities have involved members of the public in designing videos, presentations, cartoons and performances to express their views and communicate them to a wider audience (see Chapter 6).

49

Open-space events

'Open space' is a technique for working with groups in a very informal space which offers an opportunity for participants to discover and build their own shared agenda (see Chapter 6).

Closed simulations

These are often used to try and predict the future, using computer models of how systems will function, and enabling participants to explore the implications of changes in one or more of the variables. Computer and business games are a variant of closed simulations.

Open simulations

These have been developed as a tool to help multiple stakeholders engage in learning from the future. A one- to three-day event creates the conditions and features of a potential future in which participants can learn about how they and other participants might respond. There are few rules, and players are allowed to draw on their own real life experiences to shape action in the future, and then to plan real life action in the present in response to what they have learnt. The work of Laurie McMahon and colleagues at the Office for Public Management has contributed significantly to the development of open simulations as a useful tool for public managers (see Chapter 6).

Open negotiations

Open negotiations are another approach developed by Laurie McMahon and colleagues at the Office for Public Management. They take the idea of an interactive workshop a stage further, and enable groups of stakeholders to work together for one or two days to carry out all the negotiations necessary to reach a decision. They require considerable advance preparation to ensure that people are 'ready to negotiate' and it is important that all the key players are present, and have the authority to act. However, they can offer an exciting acceleration of what is often a time-consuming process of checking back and deliberating over several months before action is taken.

Judging/deciding together

Deliberative polls

A deliberative opinion poll is the approach pioneered by Professor James Fishkin, which has been used in the USA both at national level for the presidential election and at local level (Fishkin, 1995). A representative sample of around 250 to 600 people meet over two, three or four days. An initial opinion poll of participants establishes the baseline opinion of the group. There are then a number of opportunities for exploration and small-group discussion. Participants can ask questions of stakeholders, with the answers shared with other participants. Another poll is taken at the end of the discussion to see how and whether views have changed. The greatest drawback is the cost of bringing so many people together for several days (see Chapter 4).

Citizens' juries

Citizens' juries are, as the name suggests, a process that involves a relatively small group of people in a deliberative process over several days to reach a conclusion about an issue of local government or public policy. The jury has usually around 12 to 20 members, and meets over four or five days. There is an independent moderator to help the jury processes run smoothly, and the jury sometimes has an advocate to help the questioning and discussion. The jury hears evidence from a variety of expert witnesses, and can ask for further information or clarification. Once the jury has heard all the evidence, it draws up its conclusions in a report to the council. The LGMB has been influential in piloting and evaluating citizens' juries and the results were published in a report *Citizens Juries in Local Government* by Hall and Stewart. The relatively elaborate nature of juries makes it important that the issue chosen is sufficiently carefully defined to make a jury effective, and that prior consideration has been given at both political and managerial level to the extent that they are able to recognize the legitimacy of the jury and to give sufficient weight to their findings in planning future action. Several juries have reported findings which have not been implemented, and while they offer powerful learning, it can be counter-productive if they are then ignored (see Chapter 4).

Community workshops/community issues groups

These are both methods developed by the Office for Public Management in response to some of the problems related to citizens' juries. They use the same deliberative approach, but are less intensive. Community workshops enable a group of people to meet over a longer period of time, rather than in a concentrated few days, and to work together to reach conclusions. The community workshop is shorter, and is drawn from a relatively homogeneous group of the population to help them to work together quickly. The workshops are facilitated to help groups of people clarify their thinking and perspectives by talking issues through with others who share some experience, and then to help form recommendations or suggestions. Workshops are often run in clusters to enable a wide range of different perspectives to be gathered, and then it is possible to hold further sessions where different workshops groups exchange views and test out possible solutions (see Chapter 4).

Consensus conferences

Consensus conferences have been used in Denmark as a more informal process of bringing citizens together to hear the views of various experts and to try and reach some consensual view. They can involve a panel of 10 or 20 people who prepare in much the same way as a citizens' jury, learning necessary background knowledge, preparing questions, choosing experts to call as witnesses and so forth. Once they have heard witnesses, a report is drawn up. This sort of approach can be useful if technical or scientific issues are under consideration (Stewart, 1995).

The term 'consensus conference' is also used to describe an event towards the end of a consultation process where different groups of stakeholders, or people who have been involved in dialogue at earlier stages, are brought together in a facilitated workshop to try and agree a way forward. This may involve negotiation between groups, or a shared process of option appraisal based on options generated at earlier stages. It helps if the ground rules for participation in a consensus conference enable individuals to 'represent' organizations and groups, and to commit their organization to the next steps that are agreed.

Delegating/supporting

There are many examples of service users managing their own affairs including tenant management organizations, co-operatives, community development trust and user self-help groups. Three important methods of delegating decisions to citizens more generally are:

1. Town/estate plans

Town or estate plans are developed by the key community representatives and agencies in a geographical area. They often involve several stages of problem identification and consultation, but the key is a process whereby the people who live on an estate or in a village or town are involved in deciding the actions that should be taken. The plan is then 'signed off' by all the agencies who have to make it work. A key to success is the extent to which communities and agencies feel 'held to account' for delivering the plan. In some circumstances, this takes the form of a contract or agreement to deliver.

2. Delegation to neighbourhood committees

A number of authorities have set up local committees to which some decision-making, and some funding is delegated. These initiatives vary considerably, however, and they do not all involve the delegation of decision-making to local people. Some are dominated by councillors, and some are only advisory bodies although there is some evidence that simply having a forum for local conversation can be powerful in influencing wider policies. Increasingly, neighbourhood organizations are becoming real decision-making forums, and are beginning to involve other agencies such as health, education and so forth. Many of the new action zones involve the setting up of new management arrangements for the zones which involve local people. The new primary care groups involve at least one lay member of the public in decision-making about primary care. Walsall, Norwich, Lambeth and many other local authorities are setting up neighbourhood or area forums.

3. Referendums/citizen ballots

One way to engage the public in decision-making is by referendum or citizen ballot. These have seldom been used in Britain at local government level, but their use is likely to expand as a result of the new local government legislation. Ballots about desirability of a local mayor may become common, as may referenda on local plans. The most interesting local referendum was held in Milton Keynes recently, where citizens chose a higher level of council tax in order to preserve services.

Surveys and engagement

Claire Cowley

INTRODUCTION

Local authorities have been using surveys – a systematic collection and analysis of data – for many years now, for corporate monitoring and tracking purposes. Even with the increasing use of new and innovative qualitative (exploratory and deliberative) techniques for consulting and involving the public in decision-making (some of which are described later in this book), the survey methodology remains the backbone of many local authorities' consultation processes.

However, the thinking has not generally been paralleled in survey methods, which remain in use as research, rather than consultation and involvement, tools. This chapter explores where survey methodologies can be used effectively in local authorities, but also considers where techniques can be advanced to not only conduct 'pure' research, but involve residents more fully in decision-making and begin to engage them in local democratic renewal.

THE USE OF SURVEYS IN LOCAL GOVERNMENT

Residents' opinion surveys – characteristics and benefits

The main survey research project that many local authorities conduct regularly is the residents' opinion poll. These studies are generally carried out face-to-face in respondents' homes. Commissioned from one of the main market research agencies, or in a few authorities carried out using in-house resources, these projects are a means of providing a corporate overview of service use, satisfaction and performance.

As it would not be cost- or resource-effective to consult everyone in a local authority area in this way, a sampling approach must be decided on. Typically, around 1,000 residents are polled to ensure sufficient overall reliability of results, and the ability to analyse by subgroups. Random sampling would be the best method to use to maximize this reliability, but again, for cost and resource reasons, this method is not often employed.

Interviewees are generally selected using a quota system, where enumeration districts (subdivisions) of a local authority ward are sampled and the demographic profile of those districts supplied to interviewers, so respondents selected match the profile of the district. When results are collated they are checked for their overall representativeness, and weighted back to the true population profile if necessary.

The questionnaire used for such a survey typically includes mostly 'closed' questions, where respondents select their answer from a pre-coded list as the following example shows:

Question (a)   *Which of the following best describes you when it comes to voting in local council elections?*

I always vote
I usually vote
I sometimes do and sometimes do not vote
I usually do not vote
I never vote

The options the respondent has to choose from are shown on a card separate from the questionnaire. Closed questions can include a variety of types of design, including 'agree/disagree' statements, ranking factors in order of preference, satisfaction scales (very/fairly satisfied, neither/nor, very fairly dissatisfied) and so on.

Questionnaires can also include open questions, although as these are less straightforward and more expensive to analyse, they tend to be limited in number in most tracking surveys. Open questions might include examples such as the following, if respondents to question (a) above said that they did vote at least sometimes:

Question (b)   *Please describe to me what it is that makes you want to vote in local council elections?*

The respondent is then free to give an unprompted verbatim response.

Mixing types of questions means that a wide range of topics can be covered. Such surveys generally cover residents' use of, and satisfaction with, the range of services the council provides, and their perceived importance. Questions are also likely to cover residents' perceptions of the council generally, local democracy issues, priorities for local authority action, views on information and communication, and questions regarding the authority's future policy decisions and direction. Example one shows the range of questions asked recently by a local authority in their annual residents' survey. They are selected from throughout the questionnaire, which ran to 30 numbers in total.

Example one – example questions from a recent local authority residents' opinion survey

Q (a) and (b)   *What are the three or four most important issues facing you or your family/this local authority area?*

Open questions

Q   *Have you got in touch with your local councillor in the last year?*

Closed question – yes/no

Q   *What is your local councillor's name?*

Interviewer codes from list of current councillors

Q (a)   *Looking at this list of services that the council provides,which do you think are provided well?*

Q (b)   *And which do you think need to be improved?*

Q   *How satisfied or dissatisfied are you with (each of them)?*

Showcard list of services

Q   *Thinking now about the information the council provides, how important is it that the council informs residents on what it is doing and why?*

Pre-coded answers (very, fairly, not very, not at all important)

The main advantages of a survey of this kind are as follows:

- involves wide coverage of the population of a local authority area;
- representative of the population as a whole, and its subgroups;
- quantitative (numerical) data gathered can be analysed statistically to look at differences between subgroups, and trends over time.

Statistical measurement of this kind enables councils to be confident that a certain proportion of the population holds a particular view. In some cases, this factor is especially important to local politicians, in legitimizing particular decisions that may be unpopular with certain sections of a community.

The representative nature of surveys is seen as particularly important to many local authorities in reinforcing the democratic imperative – that the consultation they are carrying out is broad-based and inclusive, and representative of the community they serve. In the same way, subgroups of the population can be reliably represented and their views can be compared. What do young people think about public transport reliability in the area compared to those who are middle-aged? What about information provision in the borough – are high-income households happier than those with lower incomes? A wealth of information can be gathered on these matters and many others included in the questionnaire.

Surveys like this do not only provide absolute answers from the population at a point in time. Information can also be gleaned as to relative satisfaction with certain services when compared with others within the council, those of other local authorities (if comparable information is available) and in previous years' polls.

All these factors are accepted advantages of corporate surveys, and rightly so. The ability to gauge and track opinion about all council services, year after year, can be extremely useful for monitoring and forward planning, helping with decisions as to where to target resources, and bringing service managers closer to the views of the public they work for.

Other local authority survey projects

Corporate residents' opinion polls are often the most high-profile – and time- and resource-intensive – survey projects within local authorities. Of course, other surveys are conducted by councils, such as studies among specific user groups (or non-user groups), sections of the community, particular areas of the authority and so on.

Many local authorities with responsibility for social housing conduct regular tenants' surveys covering satisfaction with the home and specific aspects of it, questions on repairs and maintenance provision, information and communication and rent setting. Again, these monitoring and tracking surveys can be helpful in implementing changes to the service received on the basis of views expressed. These questions can be included in a general residents' survey, depending on the total proportion of tenants in a population, but more detailed questions are often asked separately.

Other sections of the population can be surveyed by authorities when a particular input is needed from a group, or it is felt that the views of a discrete section of the community are not often expressed. For example, surveying businesses, older or younger people, or parents whose children go to local authority schools in the area, can enable local authorities to ask them about topics that cannot be covered by a broader residents' attitude survey.

Smaller surveys can be useful to individual directorates or service heads if changes are being proposed to a service or area, or if information already gathered needs to be supplemented with more detail.

Techniques used for smaller surveys of this kind, where the questions asked are particular to a service or area, should be designed with the population to be surveyed in mind. Face-to-face and telephone methods are relatively expensive to use but elicit higher response rates. Telephone surveying is quick and particularly appropriate to certain audiences (eg business) but may miss out certain groups of people who are not on landline phones. Postal surveys generally only give reliable results when a subject is of enough interest for respondents to reply in sufficient numbers and across different demographic groups.

The boxes below give examples of uses of surveys in local government, where resources and issues under consideration have merited substantially different approaches, but where results have been used similarly in developing and improving services or changing policy. In addition, some examples show where surveys can be used alongside other techniques to maximize the availability of useful management information.

Example two – uses of different approaches in survey research

Local recycling survey

Residents in a trial recycling area were mailed a questionnaire on their views on the scheme. Because of effective advance publicity and local interest in the scheme, the response was relatively high. The survey process itself provided further information to residents about the scheme. The project was followed up by changes to the service as a result of views expressed, alongside a physical survey of recycling material collected, to examine ways to maximize recycling opportunities. The study proved a cost-effective way of gathering and sharing information.

Young people's survey

As part of an urban authority's commitment to consulting widely with different sectors of the community, young people aged 14–18 were surveyed through local schools and colleges. Issues expressed were explored at a youth conference the following year and specific policy and service areas concerning young people were addressed. A youth panel has also been set up as a permanent channel through which young people can voice their concerns. Although a considerable cost was attached to all these activities, robust data was gathered and the consultation process taken seriously by young people, council officers and members.

Beef in school meals

A need was identified for a widespread and quick consultation about beef on school menus after the BSE alarm. A telephone survey was conducted among residents and parents on the issue, which resulted in beef being taken off the menu. Although relatively expensive, this method brought quick results from a representative sample of the population.

Survey work can also be supplemented by other methods of data collection and consultation. Desk research on earlier studies, whether local or national, can be helpful in gaining comparable results. The design of surveys can be aided by conducting qualitative research, or consultation with front-line staff as to key issues of concern. If surveys bring to light issues in need of further research work, then qualitative work can be conducted to elucidate survey findings.

POTENTIAL PROBLEMS OF SURVEY RESEARCH

As illustrated above, survey techniques can be extremely useful to local authorities in elucidating and clarifying residents' attitudes. However, the problems inherent in using surveys are often overlooked; polling is not a 'catch-all' technique or a panacea of public consultation.

Probably the most obvious disadvantage of surveys is the time and resources they require to manage successfully. For corporate residents' surveys, from design and commissioning to reporting and action planning, the survey process can take up the best part of a year. Care needs to be taken that sufficient internal resources are allocated to these aspects, as well as general project management. Another possible disadvantage of the survey method is lack of representativeness. If quota sampling returns are not monitored carefully, or the sample frame used in a project is incomplete or out of date, samples achieved can be skewed or inaccurate. Researchers can run the risk at the very least of offending residents (eg where people have died since a customer database was last updated) and, in particular, producing findings that are not representative of the current population.

In addition, response rates gained by surveys need to be monitored to ensure adequate coverage of the population. This is a particular problem with postal survey research, where respondents effectively select themselves. Even with quota surveys, though, or those with a preselected sample, response rates vary widely depending on the subject matter and other factors. Response rates can be as low as 30 per cent, even to face-to-face quota samples, for example on estates with entryphone access.

In this way, no sample on which a survey is based is going to be perfect. Compromises as to the reliability of the data will often have to be made, trading these off against other decisions as to methodology or cost. Survey managers need to have enough experience and knowledge of these pitfalls to make their survey a success, although often local authorities do not have access to internal research departments and may fall back on making 'best guesses' as to methodological approaches.

The use of a questionnaire as a survey tool has disadvantages of its own. Questions may be designed by 'distant' researchers/officers, with little input from residents. As questions are generally closed, detail and depth can be lacking from answers, which can frustrate the service manager, who asks, 'So why did they say that?'

These disadvantages can be countered to some extent by incorporating open questions into the survey and also by conducting pre-survey qualitative research to feed into questionnaire design but this 'designer bias' will still exist, and has to be acknowledged. Following from this, respondents may not be in a position to answer questions fully, because of a lack of information or inability to discuss or debate the issue. Example three illustrates this problem.

Example three – scenario illustrating a potential problem with survey research

Two respondents are posed the question:

'How satisfied are you with care services for the elderly?'

An older respondent, in sheltered accommodation herself, might say:

'Well, overall, quite satisfied, but I hate the replacement carer I get when my own is away and the indignity of having my laundry taken away to be washed. I do love the food though'.

So, her answer would be coded as 'fairly satisfied' although her view is mixed.

Another, younger respondent, could be asked the same question, to ascertain the wider community's views of care for the elderly, as he has said that a relative is in care in the council area:

'I don't really know – I think this council is quite good at that sort of thing – my gran's in a home and she quite likes it' (although the home is in the next county and privately owned!)

So, his answer would also be 'fairly satisfied', given through a 'top of mind' response and limited access to facts, and refering to a home which is not run by a local authority.

This example shows the potential pitfalls in failing to expand up people's views given in a questionnaire. Although good questionnaire design can temper these problems to a certain extent, researchers do have to bear these problems in mind when considering how thoroughly an issue or problem has, in fact, been covered.

In addition, respondents may well display unwillingness to disclose information to a survey researcher. Perhaps they feel a lack of affinity with the council as an institution, or that their views will not be taken seriously or acted up. There is little that can be done by a local authority to counter this in the short term, but steps taken by an authority to communicate its commitment to involving the public may change views in the longer term.

DEVELOPING SURVEY RESEARCH – STARTING AN EXCHANGE WITH RESIDENTS

Continuing this theme, a problem seen as fundamental to survey research even by practitioners, and one that is often discussed but rarely addressed, is the fact that survey research does not aid dialogue or discussion. The relationship between the 'researcher' and the 'researched' is essentially an unequal, paternalistic one. Just as deliberative consultation and engagement techniques allow those involved to debate and challenge issues under consideration, survey techniques allow for very little of this interplay between those with influence – the commissioners and researchers – and those without – the public or residents in a local authority area.

This was not considered to be especially important until the focus of local governance fell less on the resident as a consumer of services, and more on the citizen, with a right to information, a voice and for that voice to be heard. With the increasing emphasis on local democratic renewal and involvement, this lack of interplay between service providers, users, and the wider community, has hastened such a critique of survey methods. However, because such 'mass interaction' survey research is still the most effective way for local authorities to allow large numbers of residents to talk to them directly, methods are beginning to be explored of making this research as valuable an exchange of views as possible.

At the very least, it is relatively easy for local authorities to consider what to do alongside surveys to bolster their success. Communication to respondents, and the wider community at the outset of a survey project, helps throw open the project to the public – letting people know that the council is consulting and listening. Eye-catching articles in the council newspaper or editorializing/ spreads in the local press can help to inform people about what consultation is happening, why it is taking place and what will happen as a result.

Feeding back to residents

A local authority which had been conducting a residents' opinion survey for some years recently extended its consultation strategy to include a feedback mechanism. After the survey had been analysed and the results presented to committee, a centrespread of the survey results was published in the council newspaper, and delivered free to all households in the area. It detailed the main findings and put them in the context of proposed actions by the council and budgetary decisions. It also included information about other consultation activities planned by the council in the future.

The same council used a similar approach with its annual tenants' survey, reporting the results and proposals for action in the tenants' magazine. It was reported together with other initiatives used to consult tenants in the area.

Such communication can be seen as the continuation of a dialogue which starts with the survey research itself. If a framework for further comments and feedback from respondents is invited, this further extends the dialogue and exchange. In addition, respondents can be asked whether they want to take part in follow-up group discussions on issues which may need further clarification and depth of treatment, and whether they want to be consulted again on the issues concerned.

It is also important to establish a feeling of trust and rapport with past, present and future respondents. If residents see that actions result from them having given their views, they may well be more likely to take part in such exercises in the future. In a small but significant way, they are likely to feel that their local authority is trying to do its best for them with the council tax money that they pay every year.

Of course, it may be inappropriate to share some consultation findings, especially those on sensitive issues. However by normalizing marketing as part of the survey process and working closely with PR and communication functions, local authorities can start to establish two-way communication with residents and increase understanding and legitimacy of local governance processes.

USING A PANEL APPROACH

So, an argument can be presented for a more thoughtful, creative use of surveys and techniques which could accompany them. Establishing a residents' panel is one way of standardizing these feedback and exchange processes, as well as providing a representative 'pool' of residents who are willing to be involved in consultation on various issues. It is a method that is being used by an increasing number of local authorities. Research panels can offer any combination of the following advantages:

- the collection of survey data from a representative cross-section of residents:
    - similar to *ad-hoc* surveys, rigorous sampling;
    - representative, input from large numbers, all sections of community;
    - survey interviews, measurement and statistical analysis;
- a database of 'community contacts':
    - easy and cost-effective communication for future surveys;
    - ability to choose from a wide range of survey methodologies;
        postal, telephone, face-to-face, Internet;
        full sample or subsets;
    - ability to develop a reciprocal relationship with participants;
- a framework for community consultation:
    - draw on wider engagement methodologies;
        focus groups;
        deliberative small group events (eg community workshops, citizens' juries, issues groups etc);
        large group events (eg community mapping, whole systems events such as visioning, community conferences etc);
        open fora such as neighbourhood fora, user fora, council events;
- 'magnet' for the development of partnerships across council departments and across local public service agencies:
    - able to attract interest and funding from departments, and from other agencies such as NHS trusts, health authority, police, colleges;
    - create a mechanism to link up issues (such as community safety, social exclusion etc) across agencies.

Which of these arise as outcomes will depend to a certain extent on how the panel is recruited, managed and maintained. The following section deals with these methodological issues in some depth, as this detail is crucial when it comes to setting up a panel.

Issues of representativeness in panel research

Quality recruitment of citizens' panels is essential to ensure that the 'pool' of residents is representative of the population at large; as in a sample survey, it will effectively be mirroring that population in consultation exercises. Postal, face-to-face and telephone methodologies have all been used by local authorities in setting up their panels. Each method has advantages and disadvantages, and as in any decision about research and consultation, the method best aligned to the purpose, circumstances in the authority and resources available should be chosen.

Many local consultation panels – including City of York and Calderdale and Kirklees (jointly funded by Kirklees and Calderdale Councils and the health authority) – have used the postal methodology to initially recruit, and then consult residents. Invitations to join the panel are sent out to a random sample of the electoral roll, along with a recruitment questionnaire to record demographic details about the respondent. The panel is then formulated from these responses. Bradford have used GP lists as a sample frame; mailouts were targeted to 25,000 people when setting up the panel, with an achieved panel database of 25,000. This is a relatively cheap method to employ, and can be targeted geographically to ensure that all local authority areas are represented. In addition, as responses initially are by post, in the future people may be more likely to respond to a postal questionnaire than those recruited by other methods. Postal recruitment does, however, elucidate a relatively poor response rate of 10–15 per cent, and introduces an element into the recruitment process of self-selection. It is more likely to be successful in non-inner city areas, or where the population is more stable (ie fewer people moving house) and where additional 'top-up' recruitment can be employed.

Telephone recruitment produces a better response – 35–40 per cent – and can be conducted in a much shorter time frame. The Lewisham and Arun panels have used this technique. By setting specific recruitment controls, such as for age, sex, work status, ethnicity, tenure and others, a representative panel can be recruited over a relatively short time period. It is also possible, and advisable, to add to the recruitment module a set of substantive consultation questions to maximize value for money. Telephone recruitment is more expensive than postal recruitment. In addition, not every resident is on the telephone, and telephone ownership is lower among some groups. However, telephone recruitment offers good geographical coverage, since contacts can be spread right across the borough.

Face-to-face recruitment – contacting potential panel members in their own homes – increases costs even further. This type of recruitment does benefit from the personal contact between recruiter and potential panel member, which helps to ensure good participation rates. It is also easier to control geographical and other recruitment factors through the face-to-face approach. If an authority already conducts an annual residents' survey, costs can be substantially reduced by 'piggy-backing' recruitment questions on to the questionnaire.

However, it is likely to produce a more clustered panel, since interviewers will tend to work in predetermined geographical areas such as enumeration districts. Response rates may not be any better than those gained in a tele-phone recruitment exercise. In addition, when follow-up panel surveys are carried out, the methodology used is no longer face-to-face, but generally postal or telephone. This can have a detrimental effect on the response and drop-out rates.

So recruitment decisions will have to be made as a 'trade-off' with other factors. Panel size and balancing options will also involve this weighing up. Any survey research depends on the sample responding to a particular project being representative of the community overall. However, differential and sometimes unpredictable response rates to panel projects will mean that the size of the panel will have to be significantly higher than the eventual sample size required to ask questions. If, for example, an eventual sample size of 1,000 people is required for a particular project, then at the very least the panel size will have to be 1,300 for adequate responses from telephone surveys, and higher when using postal consultation. In addition, if representation of particular groups of the population on the panel is important (eg younger people, Asian people), the overall panel size may have to be increased to allow a proportional subgroup on the panel, a larger 'booster' group of these residents to be included, or extra recruitment using different methods employed (face-to-face, recruitment through local networks/community groups etc).

Even taking these factors into account, it is likely that the broad representativeness of the panel will be lessened in each survey project as certain groups of the population (older people, those in the ABC1 social groups) are more likely to respond than others. As a result, responses are likely to have to be weighted back to the true panel make-up to compensate.

It is these, and related issues, that mean that a truly representative research panel is hard to achieve in the long term. The time and money spent in regularly revisiting the 'balance' of the panel, and conducting extra recruitment activities to this end, can drain the resources of already strained consultation budgets. In addition, there can be some concern that panel members can be 'conditioned' into certain patterns of behaviour and response by their participation.

Because of these factors, and modernizing imperatives which push for wider and deeper consultation with local residents, some local authorities have combined the use of annual or biannual residents' surveys with panel activity. Regular 'tracking' style surveys are still the best way of being able to carry out research on views on services, communications, policy and democracy issues which require the council to have asked the whole community, not that subsection which has opted to be consulted through agreeing to a longer-term panel commitment.

Panels and surveying

Panel research, therefore, can be used by a council to gauge views on issues of a more *ad-hoc* nature; specific aspects of a service, perhaps, which are to be changed and on which consultation is needed. Service managers receive the information they require in a cost-effective but relatively quick way, without having to arrange survey activity independently. Costs can be brought down even further by working with partner agencies.

Councils using a panel approach have found that they have been able to consult on a variety of issues which might have been excluded if a tracking approach alone were used. This is increasingly important with the imperative for a local authority to consult extensively on existing service provision and proposed changes. Issues covered by the Kirklees panel include shopping patterns, highway maintenance, communicating with the public, housing needs, transport and environmental issues and future priorities. Bradford's panel has recently covered public safety in parks, the community safety and crime and disorder bill and housing issues, among others. It is possible that consultation around these areas may not have taken place without the panel, or at the very least it would have been less time- and cost-effective.

The example in the box below shows the issues covered by the City of York Council's panel in a year – a wide variety of subjects which might have been left off the corporate consultation 'list' if a residents' survey had been the only method used to consult the local community.

Issues covered by CYC's Talk About panel in a year

- life in York/living standards
- policing;
- crime and safety;
- affordable housing;
- public transport;
- park and ride;
- child-friendly issues;
- access to local information;
- planning applications;
- leisure provision;
- contracting out of services/possibilities for private finance;
- school meals;
- street lighting;
- poverty/social exclusion;
- pavement maintenance and repair;
- parks and open spaces;
- discharge procedures from the local hospital;
- European finance;
- millennium celebrations;
- issues covered in future surveys.

These issues were not exclusively covered in survey research. Focus groups and workshops were also used, both as stand-alone projects and where survey findings needed clarification or exploration. In addition, some research concentrated on particular user groups (eg parents with children at York schools for school meals consultation).

Panels and engagement

So, we have seen that panel survey research can be conducted to give user and citizen views on services and policies. The way that consultation can be carried out enables residents to be engaged in council processes of decision-making to a greater extent than an annual survey can allow. Contact with the panel on a regular basis allows panel members to feel more involved in the consultative process than if they were involved in a one-off survey. The very act of continuing questioning makes people feel that their views are of note and are being taken into account in a two-way dialogue. Mechanisms that can be put in place to run alongside the panel can heighten this feeling of engagement and involvement, and that decisions are being taken in the light of residents' views.

The panellists' relationship with the local authority can be conceived as that of a contract – that panellists are charged with a responsibility to fill in questionnaires or take part in a certain amount of consultation exercises, but that in return there will be some feedback as to what they have said collectively, and how their views are being taken into account. Newsletters can be sent to respondents telling them of initiatives and actions taken as a result of their views. Reporting in the local press can also be used in this way, thus panellists can be drawn into the 'net' of council processes. They become aware of local council initiatives and more informed about local democracy generally. They may even, depending on events and consultation exercises run by the panel sponsors, be able to meet officers and members and question them directly. In this way, members of the public build a very different relationship with the council.

Lewisham is an example of an authority which has used its panel in this way, to involve citizens directly in the decision-making and policy-formation processes of the council. In addition to using surveying techniques for *ad-hoc* questioning of all panel members and smaller subgroups, panellists have also participated in qualitative group events about council and partner service provision and information, but also in decisions about policy direction and new initiatives. Using some of the deliberative techniques mentioned in Chapter 4, panel members have been able to debate issues around education policies, future leisure strategies and political management structure of the council, among others. Kirklees' and Arun's panel members have also been involved in events of this kind, as the box below shows.

Involving panellists in qualitative consultation and deliberation

Panel members in Lewisham were involved in a two-day community discovery event on 'making the connections' between different local public services. The purpose was to enable residents to explore and then map relationships between themselves, public services and wider community resources, and to describe how these combine to achieve health, learning and safety for themselves and the wider community. The findings were used by the council in planning more 'joined-up' service delivery in the future, and were also published by the Public Management Foundation (Parston and Cowe, 1998).

Members of Kirklees' Talkback panel have been involved in a similar way in qualitative and deliberative projects, which have included focus groups on service access and a scrutiny commission for older people. The latter involved older panel members being mailshotted, a certain number recruited and hearing evidence in a 'jury-like' setting as to service provision for older people. The commission's recommendations have been accepted by full council.

Arun panel members took part in a consultative forum on the regeneration of Bognor Regis. A day-long event included people recruited from the panel being involved in debating proposals for development in the town. For example, representatives from two proposed marina developments acted as 'witnesses' for the event and were quizzed by panel members on their proposed schemes. Representatives from the council, local businesses and the local paper were also invited to give their perspective. The day was reported on partly through a full council meeting on the future of Bognor, when panel members were invited to feed proceedings back to members.

There has been some criticism regarding the use of a panel methodology to engage local populations in increased contact and exchange with a local authority. This criticism has rested on two premises: (1) that closer involvement– engagement with the council leads to panellists becoming 'unrepresentative' of the population at large; and (2) that only a small minority of people will, in fact, be engaged in this way and that closer involvement is a false premise on which to base a panel consultation strategy.

Some local authorities cite the first point to suggest caution in adopting a panel approach. Others, though, say that this is a positive effect – that more and more people will be in contact with the council and have their views changed about what happens within the walls of the town hall.

Often, authorities holding this view use panel research in conjunction with other consultation. Panel research can be usefully combined with regular tracking of opinion across a local authority area. In this case, it can be argued, *ad-hoc* gauging of views through panel survey research, and the use of qualitative and deliberative methods to explore issues in more detail, can be seen as complementary to the 'finer' measurement of opinion associated with tracking.

Indeed, it is patronizing, and a false premise in itself, to think that the 'norm' of interaction is through asking many people their 'top of mind' view through survey research. By only carrying out this type of research, we can only skim the surface of people's views, and do not achieve the depth of debate and exchange that is achieved in other realms of people's lives. By supplementing survey methods with other ways of exploring residents' aspirations and experiences, councils can begin to ask residents to make a truly meaningful contribution to decision-making.

The second point above may also be true at the beginning of a panel's life span, but as many local authorities do very little at the moment to involve residents, it could be said that doing little is better than doing nothing at all. In addition, refreshing panel membership on a regular basis and involving more and more people in qualitative and deliberative events opens the 'consultation net' more widely and spreads the message abroad about the council being willing to involve local residents. Used in conjunction with an effective PR and communications strategy, and other methods of involving the public (neighbourhood meetings, user fora and so on), residents can be effectively engaged in council processes and able to conduct a dialogue with local officers and councillors.

In addition to the engagement of panellists, local partners' relationships with the council can also be strengthened. Several local authorities have been active in using panels to facilitate partnerships (eg Lewisham, Kirklees, Bradford). In Lewisham, through a regular steering group meeting and contact between lead officers and partner contacts, research and consultation activity is scoped, progress reports shared and thus informal networks strengthened. On issues such as community safety, health, lifelong learning and social cohesion, research activities can be co-ordinated and streamlined. The steering group approach can also facilitate internal partnership working, bringing together officers from different departments to work towards a coherent approach to panel consultation. However, partnership approaches do not have to be overly structured or timetabled, as the example in the box below shows.

Facilitating partnerships in panel consultation

Kirklees' panel is run using a partnership approach between the local and health authorities, dividing up the tasks involved and costs incurred. There is no formal steering group as such, but meetings are held when necessary. The health authority manages the database of panel members' details while the questionnaire design is the responsibility of Kirklees Council. Division of tasks other than these core responsibilities is largely on a pragmatic basis. Costs are calculated at the end of each financial year, and timetables are agreed regularly. The arrangement is an informal one but one which works well for all the partners involved. Bradford's panel is run on a similarly pragmatic basis, with responsibility for questionnaire design and co-ordination being taken on by each of the council, TEC and wealth authority in turn. Liaison is carried out by holding regular meetings between the partners.

CONCLUSION

This chapter has looked at the uses of surveys in local government, and the development of this approach by way of panel consultation. Surveys used in isolation do not tend to engage local communities or draw them closer to their local authority, but when used in conjunction with other techniques (increased information provision/feedback, continued dialogue through panel membership, panellists' engagement in processes other than surveys), this form of structured information gathering can be very useful in aiding closer involvement of local communities in decision-making.

Involvement in deliberation and decision-making

Robin Clarke

INTRODUCTION

In the last few years there has been an explosion in the usage of new forms of public engagement by local authorities and other public agencies. These new engagement tools are perhaps best symbolized by the citizens' jury, which first appeared in this country in 1996. This chapter considers why these methods have evolved, how they work and also how this new learning can best be utilized by local government.

If the pattern of public involvement in local government over the years is looked at, the picture which emerges is quite distinct. Local authorities seem relatively confident about methods which ask the public to comment on a service retrospectively, to review their experience of a particular aspect of a council's work, or they have been asked to voice an opinion on the here and now. Consultation which has asked people about the future seems less successful. The reason for this seems to be that while the public can give a meaningful response to what has already happened to them, we are often less well equipped to comment on hypothetical futures where we rarely have relevant background knowledge.

The feedback from consultation exercises about the future has often taken the form of unwieldy wish-lists at one extreme or a complete lack of aspirations at the other, both of which are often of little practical use. Asking the public to set priorities, or to choose between possible alternatives, seems particularly problematic. This is, in part, due to the use of inappropriate methods. Local authorities (and most every other public sector body for that matter) have tended to rely on a narrow range of methods, probably consisting of public meetings, attitude surveys and, increasingly frequently, focus groups. We have then proceeded to bend the methods to fit the problem at hand. As the example below demonstrates, when we seek to try and engage people in commenting on issues which they have little prior knowledge of, the responses are too often 'top of mind' with little grounding in reality.

As discussed in previous chapters, it is important that the nature of the problem/issue dictates the method. The new agenda for involving the public in helping to design their futures has presented us with a whole new series of new problems for which simple surveys and focus groups may not be appropriate.

Consider the following example. A researcher knocks on your door one evening and asks if you can spare a few minutes to take part in a survey on behalf of the local authority. The first question relates to the quality of the street lighting; you look up and down the street at the street lights and give the researcher a reply. The next question asks how you feel about the quality of refuse collection services; you look over at your bins, note that they have been emptied and there is no rubbish strewn along the street, and again reply. The third question asks you what you would prioritize additional funding between leisure, housing, education and social services. As you have not used any of the council's leisure services for several years, have never been a council tenant, having no children or experience of local schools and no contact with social services, you still give the researcher a response. Over the next few days you note articles in the local paper concerning various council services and begin to wonder about your reply to the third question.

What value should we place on these responses? Questions one and two, provide us with useful information. As the respondent could meaningfully comment on the quality of the service from his or her own experience. The response to the third question (which in practice will rarely meet with an 'I don't know' response) is based on little or no experience. It is also a free-floating opinion, subject to change in the short term. A more extreme instance of people giving a response to a question which they know nothing about comes from the USA. The University of Cincinnati ran a telephone survey asking people their opinions about the Public Affairs Act of 1975. About a third of the respondents offered the researchers a response voicing support or opposition to the Act. The Public Affairs Act of 1975 has never existed. There is no reason to suppose that the British public would act in a particularly different way to the US public on such an issue (Fishkin, 1995: 82).

Rather than free-floating opinion, what we should look for, particularly when considering the weighty issues such as priority setting, is more considered and stable opinion. The US social scientist Daniel Yankelovich uses the term 'public judgement' to define this: '...(public judgement) exhibits more thoughtfulness, more weighing of alternatives, more genuine engagement with the issue, more taking into account of a wide variety of factors than ordinary public opinion as measured in opinion polls' (Yankelovich, 1991: 5).

This focus on further developing and refining how the public can have a meaningful input into the direction of their public services is part of a much wider debate concerning the health of our democracy. Yankelovich is one of a growing body of theorists, and practitioners, in both the USA and Europe, who feel that there is an urgent need to revisit the relationship between public services and their public. Over the last three years, we have seen an increasing number of people questioning the health of our own democracy in Britain. In particular, there has been much criticism levelled at the depth of the relationship between public service representatives, be they officers or members, and the public. Periodic voting for councillors, who most members of the public will never meet and probably not be able to name, may not represent a healthy representative democracy. Officers, who are often even more remote than councillors, compound the problems.

Those who would seek to address these democratic ills are not seeking to replace our form of representative democracy, but to enhance it with a renewed emphasis on participatory and deliberative democracy. There is a desire to see both an extension of opportunities for ordinary members of the public to participate in civic life and to deliberate on issues which impact upon their lives. Much of the discussion set out in this chapter outlines practical processes and examples of how people can be brought much closer to public service decision-making mechanisms. While each individual process and example is a step in the right direction, even taken as a whole, they should not be seen as a panacea.

When Yankelovich wrote about the need for greater public judgement, at a macro level he was questioning the state of democracy (in this instance the USA, but equally applicable to Britain), while at a micro level he was offering a prescription for revitalizing the system. In essence, he was calling for people to be given the space to debate issues, to be aware of the consequences of their stated opinions and to have more of a direct input into their own futures through influencing the actions of public bodies. Public judgement aims to put the public on a more equal footing with other stakeholders, such as experts, or politicians by promoting a higher quality public voice which can help improve the decision-making process and make it more inclusive. For example, public judgement would be incompatible with wish-listing, as there would be an awareness of budgetary limitations – more of one thing means less of another, given a fixed pot of money. Another way of thinking of public judgement is to see it as an informed, but not necessarily expert, opinion.

The process of working towards public judgement may be termed as 'deliberation'. Over the last few years deliberation has come to symbolize a whole school of consultation methodologies (this will be discussed later in the chapter) which seek to turn potential free-floating opinion into more stable informed opinion. The concept of deliberation may be encapsulated by three 'R's': reason, reflection and refinement. First, deliberation aims to build in

the capacity for reason. This may be thought of as the opportunity for participants in a consultation exercise to discuss issues in-depth in a face-to-face
environment, with the aid of relevant background materials where necessary.
As a consequence, rather than the rushed responses typical of survey methodologies, individuals are given the time to discuss issues with one another. Second, deliberation should provide participants with time for reflection. This is
sometimes called soak-time; it is the chance for participants to internalize the
discussions they have heard away from the often hothouse atmosphere of a
consultation room, to think them over and perhaps further discuss them with
members of their family or friends. The third 'R' is refinement and logically
follows on from reason and reflection. It is about giving participants the space
to fine-tune their opinions, or as Yankelovich's terms, 'to be aware of the consequences of what they are saying'.

The most contentious, but essential, part of the deliberation process is the
provision of information. Information is the key element in moving discussion
from the free-floating top of mind variety to the more stable type akin to public
judgement. However, any material which is provided to aid the consultation
needs to be seen to be fair and balanced, setting out all sides of any relevant
arguments. Furthermore, this information needs to be both comprehensive
and accessible. Many a consultation exercise has become unstuck because a
council has been accused of biasing the deliberations through providing a
selective overview of the various positions on an issue.

Although the remainder of this chapter largely concentrates on a series of
deliberative methods and case studies, it is more important to bear in mind
what makes the models work, rather than what each model actually is. If a particular model suits an authority's purpose then it makes sense to use it. However, if none of the models appear to fit their purpose, but informed opinion is
sought, then the principles of deliberation can quite easily be applied to create
new tailor-made models.

The introduction of deliberative methodologies is often wrongly portrayed as
a fairly recent development. It is more accurate to say that their introduction into
this country is recent. Deliberation has a much longer history in other parts of the
world, particularly in North America and Scandinavia (the idea in its purest form
dates back to ancient Greece!). Citizens' juries, for example, which have created
quite a stir in this country since their introduction in 1996, have been used in the
USA for nearly 30 years, and in Germany, a variation on the theme, *plannungzelle*
(planning cells) have been around for slightly longer.

At present, relatively few of the deliberative methods designed and prac-
tised abroad have been introduced into this country, but those which have are
being enthusiastically embraced by a growing number of local authorities and
other public agencies. The following section describes three models which
taken together broadly cover the deliberative spectrum: the citizens' jury; the
community issues group; and the community workshop (Figure 4.1).

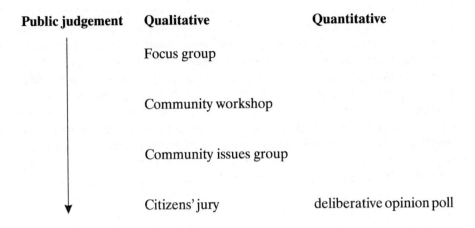

Figure 4.1 The deliberative family

THE CITIZENS' JURY AND DELIBERATIVE OPINION POLL

The citizens' jury is probably the most well-known deliberative technique in this country, not least because of its rather grand-sounding title. Since they were initially piloted in 1996, they have become an integral part of the public involvement tool-kit for many authorities. Of the various deliberative tools available, the citizens' jury is also probably the most sophisticated in terms of the depth of the public voice which can be elicited. A way of plotting juries and other deliberative techniques in terms of depth is to think of a continuum in which models increase in sophistication as we move from left to right (Figure 4.2).

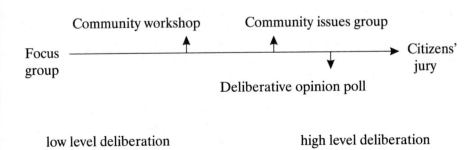

Figure 4.2 The citizens' jury

Citizens' juries were originally designed to involve ordinary members of the public, not experts, politicians, or just service users or members of interest groups, in making recommendations on quite complex issues of policy or planning. The jurors, of which there are usually 12–16, sit over four or five days (although there have been a number of successful two-day juries). They are aided in their deliberations by the provision of information, mainly through witness presentations. By the end of the process, the jurors are expected to draw up, with the aid of moderators, a series of recommendations which are then presented to the commissioning body. The commissioning body agrees to respond to these recommendations in public and say whether they plan to take them forward or not.

There are a number of stages which need careful planning if a citizens' jury is to be a success. Perhaps the most important of these is the selection of the jurors themselves. The selection criteria for any jury at the very least should include age, gender, social class, ethnicity, housing tenure and geographical spread. A jury of 12–16 people can never be representative of a local population, and any claims that they are should be treated with scepticism. What 12–16 carefully selected jurors should aim to be is a best fit, or a microcosm of the local population.

Some people have questioned the jury process on the grounds of this perceived lack of representativeness. While they are right in asserting that 12–16 people cannot be statistically representative, they are on less solid ground in claiming that statistical representativeness is a prerequisite of quality consultation. Critics will claim that because of their lack of statistical validity, it is unwise to place faith in the outcomes of a jury – we cannot be sure that another group of 12–16 jurors examining the same issue would come to the same conclusions. Experience has cast doubt upon this assertion. There have been instances of parallel juries looking at the same issues which have come up with very similar sets of recommendations. There are no examples of parallel juries coming to vastly different conclusions. It should also be said that if there is a need for quantification, then a jury should not be carried out in isolation, but in parallel with other methods of consultation. However, care would have to be taken when comparing the results from different exercises; the quality of the public voice may be quite variable.

However, this argument about representativeness should really be addressed in a quite different way. First, we need to recognize and accept that to a large extent there is a trade-off between the quality of the public voice and the quantity of people we are able to involve in any consultation exercise. In an ideal world, perhaps we would like to have as many people as possible involved in consultations and for all these people to be as well informed as participants in a citizens' jury. Professor James Fishkin of the University of Texas is a strong advocate of the need to seek ways in which we can achieve both depth and breadth: '…a major part of the problem of democratic reform is how to promote mass deliberation – how to bring the people into the process under conditions where they can be engaged to think seriously and fully about public issues' (Fishkin, 1995: 14).

Fishkin concedes that full participation is impossible and looks to a representative model. His solution is the deliberative opinion poll. This seeks to achieve the statistical robustness of quantitative opinion survey while avoiding the pitfalls of free-floating public opinion. He recommends bringing a representative sample of a population to a single venue, and over several days immersing them in the issues on which they are to be polled through small group discussions and question and answer sessions with expert witnesses. After they have had the opportunity to engage with the issues they are surveyed in detail. The resulting opinions are much more informed than those elicited through standard opinion polling.

Initially, this is an extremely appealing solution to the ideal of combining quality and quantity. However, on closer inspection there are doubts whether it is a practical solution for many, if any, local authorities. The costs of bringing a representative sample of the population to one venue for several days would be prohibitively expensive. There are also doubts as to whether the process is fully inclusive as, even though the process involves face-to-face discussions, the small-group sessions may be too large for some of the more shy participants and thus not fully participatory. While reflection and refinement would be strong, reason may be somewhat curtailed as some participants may not introduce their opinions into the discussions.

If deliberative opinion polls do not offer us a solution to the perceived problem of the small numbers associated with a citizens' jury, what is the answer? First, perhaps we need to set aside our conditioned obsession with the need to quantify everything. Deliberation should not be about trying to achieve representative statistical samples; we need to move away from being so research-obsessed and look at juries and other deliberative forms from a more democratic standpoint. We should seek to raise awareness of, and build trust in, the processes among the wider population, rather than look to involve as many people as possible in such consultation exercises. The public needs to trust that the participants in, for example, a citizens' jury are acting on the wider community's behalf, and through their deliberations are making full and considered recommendations to the best of their abilities. The trust that needs to be placed in the citizens' jury model where the implications of jurors' recommendations (if taken on board) can be far-reaching, potentially impacting upon the whole of the local community, needs to be akin to trust which we place in a jury of a court of law. This may be a lofty aim and will probably not be realized unless taking part in a citizens' jury becomes a legal requirement, rather than a purely voluntary activity.

Looking at it again from a democratic standpoint, if representativeness in a statistical sense is not realizable through deliberative processes, it still needs to be achieved in other ways. This is where the role of elected representatives is of vital importance. Councillors are, or at least should be, more actively articulating the voice of the wider community (for a fuller discussion of this see Chapter 7).

One method of building up trust in the jury process is to form a steering group with a membership drawn from a broad range of stakeholders, including those who are potentially hostile to the process. In several instances, groups or individuals hostile to the jury process have criticized it by claiming that the commissioning body has biased the exercise through controlling the jury question, the agenda and choice of witnesses, and the selection of jurors. The steering group is usually the vehicle through which the question, agenda, witness selection and juror recruitment criteria are discussed. Relevant outside bodies and individuals need to have some input into the jury and feel some sense of ownership if the process is to maintain integrity.

As juries seek to involve laypeople in the discussion of quite complex policy or planning issues, it is essential that the 4–5 days of the jury are carefully structured. Jurors need to have the maximum opportunity to engage in face-to-face deliberations, utilizing reason, reflection and refinement to the fullest extent. Reason is catered for in two ways. First, jurors are educated about the issue under discussion through a balanced mix of background information papers, and witness presentation and question and answer sessions. Rather then being passive receivers of this information, they are then afforded the opportunity to fully engage with it, and use it, through a combination of small-group and plenary sessions. Reflection is not formally built into the process, but is more of a constant theme – jurors constantly reflect on what they hear not only throughout the day, but also in the evenings after deliberations have ended. Refinement is also a constant theme. At the start of the jury participants' attention is usually drawn to a set of ground rules, one of which is that 'it is OK to change your mind'. In addition, by ensuring that the jurors' recommendations are not finalized until the late morning and afternoon of the last day, jurors have maximum opportunity to refine their opinions on the basis of the fullest amount of relevant background information.

COMMUNITY ISSUES GROUPS

The community issues group (CIG) was developed in response to a perceived need. The continuum of deliberation outlined earlier placed focus groups at the far left and citizens' juries on the far right of the scale. If deliberation is thought of as occupying the whole area to the right of focus groups, the Office for Public Management felt that the area between focus groups and citizens' juries, needed to be more fully explored and new methods introduced to complement juries. While juries are extremely effective in certain specific circumstances, we felt that there are a whole host of instances where careful deliberation is required but citizens' juries are inappropriate, usually in terms of cost, practicality, time and reach.

We looked at the mechanics of deliberation as set out earlier; reason, reflection and refinement, and sought to combine them in such a way as to maximize each. Our starting model was very much the focus group methodology and the citizens' jury. One of the frequently highlighted weaknesses with focus groups is that when confronted with a complex issue, the time constraints (typically 1.5–2 hours) of a typical discussion can mean that only a surface opinion, or worse a knee-jerk reaction, is elicited. A CIG looks to build upon the focus group methodology addressing this potential weakness by reconvening the same group of people a number of times over several weeks. As with focus groups they are designed to be run in clusters, thus including a good spread of members of the community.

The number of meetings very much depends on the complexity of the issue to be discussed. The first meeting is usually very similar to that of a focus group with participants engaging in a general discussion to uncover their current experiences and opinions – to look at the here and now. More in-depth deliberation begins with the second meeting with participants starting to engage with the issue in more depth. As with a citizens' jury, they are aided in their deliberations by the provision of relevant background information in the form of briefing papers outlining differing points of view. There then follow a series of further meetings until the issue has been fully explored and recommendations have been drawn up.

The time between each meeting is how reflection is built into the process. Our experience has shown that this time between meetings (usually one week, any longer and the process may lose momentum) is used by participants to revisit the discussions they have taken part in and often read up on the subject further, or discuss it with friends and family. At the next meeting, they will often return to the previous discussions wishing to refine what they have said and/or add further opinions. It is important that this refinement time is built in at the start of each subsequent meeting.

CIGs are highly participatory, even more so than citizens' juries, because of their smaller size and more informal nature. They are also more flexible than citizens' juries allowing an issue to be explored over a number of weeks rather than cramming it into a few days. However, CIGs can rarely achieve the depth of a citizens' jury as they lack the intensity of deliberation and are not a practical forum for witness presentation sessions with their question and answer sessions.

There is an important distinction to be made between CIGs and the similar standing committee models of public involvement. The latter are often used to shadow a defined function over an unspecified and often extended period of time, for example they might look at the broad issue of community safety role of a local authority. CIGs are designed to look at more specific issues rather than service areas. For example, a CIG may be set a question, such as, 'How can we deal more effectively with crime?' A CIG should also be disbanded after recommendations have been made on the designated issue. They should not be viewed as long-term committees; there is a danger that participants in long-term involvement may go 'native', and come to identify themselves (and be identified by the wider community) as too close to the views and objectives of the commissioning body.

THE COMMUNITY WORKSHOP

This deliberative methodology was also developed by the Office for Public Management as an attempt to provide a tool in the area of the continuum between focus groups and citizens' juries. As with the CIG model, the community workshop seeks to provide more in-depth and informed opinion than is possible in a focus group, but is not as in-depth as a jury.

Our starting point was to look at both focus groups and juries and where possible to build the strengths of each into a new model. We wanted to create a deliberative tool which provided a rapid means of 'getting into the field', and a way of involving substantial numbers of people in a cost-effective manner. From the citizens' jury model we sought to preserve the processes through which it is possible to find out what a selected group of people would think about an issue if they had the necessary time and information to discuss it in depth.

A community workshop consists of between 12 and 20 people meeting for a short period, usually over one day or two evenings. As participants only meet once relatively briefly, it is important that for purposes of group dynamics that they are homogeneous. This means that participants should have similar socio-economic and/or lifestyle characteristics so that they relate to each other quickly and easily. As with focus groups and CIGs, workshops are run in clusters, and have the potential to reach many more people than other methods, such as citizens' juries. As with a jury and a CIG, the participants are set a defined issue on which to make a series of recommendations.

Each community workshop starts with a general exploration of participants' existing views and opinions, very much in the manner of a focus group. Information is then fed into the discussion by an independent moderator to enable the process to move on to a more deliberative footing. Using a 'building-block' approach, participants gradually formulate recommendations on the main subject. To enable the process to be as participatory as possible, a mixture of small-group and plenary sessions are used. While the aim is to find areas of consensus (which the process moves naturally towards), it is equally important that disagreements are clearly noted and minority opinions expected.

A community workshop approach has, like the citizens' jury, proved to be a useful forum in which to bring managers and members of the public together. Often, there can be considerable barriers between the public service providers and the public; a workshop has proved a useful process for breaking through these.

Quality public management: continuous improvement through delighting the customer

5

Jon Harvey

INTRODUCTION

Commercial organizations know that if they look after their customers it is good for business. Business gurus argue that if they become evermore focused on delighting their customers, everyone will benefit – shareholders get increased profits, staff can get higher rewards, suppliers have stable markets and customers get what they want. 'Getting things right the first time' is the credo for most commercial organizations – integrating the twin goals of effectiveness and efficiency although in quite a number of cases, only lip-service is paid.

The idea does not have the same salience in the public sector. While 'customer care' and quality approaches have gained a lot of ground, there are good reasons why a simple private sector approach will not do. The public are not simply customers, they are also citizens. Local government managers are not simply trying to sell products, sometimes they are trying to ration them, or to regulate other sectors. Nevertheless, a focus on customer needs in service delivery will be essential for survival in an era of greater user choice and power.

All public sector managers, including those in local government, have to think of their public as (in some way) customers of services. That is the main reason for the increase in the amount of time and effort that has gone into quality management in recent years. Quality management has much to assist local authority managers in their search for better services and improved social results.

This chapter summarizes the principles and practices of quality management and will look critically at the application of quality management to public organizations – highlighting the areas where the public services have much to gain and areas where new thinking is needed. It will outline good practice in the field of quality management and identify the implications of quality management to best value and public engagement.

 Task

Think about the service that you are working in. What are the different ways in which you relate to the public. Are they citizens? Are they customers? Are they both? Are they something else, such as 'compulsory customers' – such as prisoners. How does this make any difference to the way in which you engage with them?

WHY BOTHER WITH DELIGHTING THE CUSTOMER?

We begin this section by exploring the terms 'quality' and 'customer'. It helps to have agreed definitions within a council or partnership. In many places there is a 'chaos of goodwill' where everyone signs up to providing 'quality services for our customers' but as ideas are then interpreted in a thousand ways, focus, synergy and indeed strategy, fall by the wayside.

What do we mean by quality?

Sometimes quality is defined as the 'glossy' features that turn an ordinary service into a excellent one. A quality service is special, better and, in the minds of many people, necessarily more expensive. Quality is an 'extra' – something that has to be added on.

Quality management practitioners define quality in a very different way. Although there are many descriptions – 'fit for purpose', 'zero defects' and 'meeting the agreed requirements of the customer now and in the future' – (Robson, 1993) there is a common and central idea. Quality is not an 'add on' or an extra – quality is the fundamental principle that underpins all work that is done.

Consequently, the idea of 'delighting the customer' becomes the aim of everything you are in business to do. The central goal is to make sure the customer gets the service or product he or she wants – to eliminate disappointment. The customer is placed at the centre of organizational strategy. The aim is not simply that services be effective, but they should also be effective the first time (not the second or third) – immediate satisfaction and no waste (and, therefore, greater efficiency).

What do we mean by customer?

There are many definitions of 'customer'. For commercial organizations the customer can be defined as 'the person or organization paying for the service or product'. However, this definition would then only cover external customers and since one of the key ideas of quality management is that of the internal customer, then an alternative definition is required. In this way, a customer can be defined as the person or organization who 'receives the output of a process'. In this manner, chains of internal customers and suppliers work together to produce a product or service which is provided (eventually) to the external customer.

In the public sector the concept of customers is more complex. Commercial organizations always want more customers because more customers mean more business and income. However, do housing departments want more applicants, or do social services departments want more clients? Not only are more 'customers' signs, perhaps, of worsening local conditions but these 'customers' do not bring extra payments – the consequence is having to provide services to more people with no more resources. This is yet another way in which 'customers' of public services are not the same as customers of commercial organizations – users have rights, they are citizens, and the wider public (even if they are not direct users) do still need to benefit from the service. The Human Rights Act (1998) is likely to have a huge impact upon how public service regard their 'customers' and provide services to them.

The public sector has, by it very nature, a much more diverse set of 'stakeholders' who have to be satisfied or delighted. As mentioned elsewhere in this book, there are users, carers, public representatives, other agencies, national government, council taxpayers, councillors and officers – all of whom can claim to be a 'customer' of one sort or another.

There is also the relationship between public service provider and user which increasingly is becoming more akin to active partnership rather than merely passive receipt of services by the 'customer' (see, for example, the discussion of co-production in Chapter 8).

Delighting the local authority customer

Many local authorities, police forces, hospitals and government departments up and down the country have begun to apply the principles and techniques of quality management. They clearly cannot be unthinkingly applied, and within local authorities and partnerships it is important to spend time developing a more complex picture of customers that makes sense locally. However, the focus on customer wants and needs is a useful discipline – helping to ensure that the careful balancing act of meeting the needs of different stakeholders is not achieved at the expense of the immediate consumer of the service.

In local authorities, quality management is about:

- effectiveness, efficiency, equality, economy and ethics;
- working with all stakeholders as partners in co-creating local outcomes such as sustainable local economies, better health and well-being, more community safety and so forth;
- developing a new kind of public service professionalism – focused far less on provider interests and far more on user needs and wishes;
- searching for effective ways to negotiate and agree the varying interests of the stakeholders involved.

In this way, quality public management becomes the process by which a public agency agrees and then meets the requirements of all its stakeholders.

Key reasons for 'delighting the customer'

There are many other reasons why this focus on delighting the customer makes sense in local authorities:

People expect and deserve good service

The general public will make comparisons between the standards of service they receive from commercial organizations and public agencies. These expectations will also gradually creep upwards as people are encouraged to become more assertive 'customers'. Local authorities ignore such trends at their peril, as many local newspaper stories and councillors' in-trays testify.

Customer care is good public service

No matter whether a person is a service user out of choice (such as a tourist seeking information) or constraint (such as the parent of a child taken into care), or requirement (such as an applicant for planning permission), each instance will benefit from fair, efficient and courteous treatment. In many ways, 'delighting the customer' is about the rediscovery of good public service.

Good customer care is the foundation for political support

For commercial organizations, poor customer service will lead to fewer customers as word spreads with the ultimate consequence that the business will close. Local authorities are not threatened with closure in quite the same way. However, in the end local voters will assess their council by reflecting on the services that they receive or that they hear about their friends and neighbours receiving. This may well lead to certain local political parties losing the confidence of local voters (while others gain) or it may even lead to a general loss of confidence in local politics – with dangers for the future of local government. *Modernising Government* (1999) pays great attention to local council election turnouts as indicators of local political mandate.

Delighting the customer is a vehicle for organizational development

Quality public management with its focus on delighting the customer has the potential to provide the straightforward framework and language by which all members and staff can become fully engaged in modernization. Local councils can employ the principles of quality as a vehicle for bringing together often disparate departments and professions, as well as welding together front-line staff and policy-makers under a common cause. This potential for synergy will greatly assist in turning the rhetoric of modernization, best value and community engagement into practical change.

Delighting the customer is the basis for constructive community engagement

It is true that poor service can often fuel public reactions which lead people to actively protest. However, poor service can also all too easily turn into disenchantment, cynicism and a lack of engagement. The best forms of public engagement arise out of positive partnership borne of good service and not out of professional paternalism or poor service.

Unless the public receive a service that they regard as quality there is unlikely to be much partnership, engagement or co-production. In order to achieve effective levels of public engagement (or even just making consultation work well), the public has to be delighted enough to be prepared to bother. The delivery of basic services that are timely, efficient and effective is the first step towards almost everything else the council wants to achieve. It earns the authority a right to play a leadership role in wider community affairs.

Delighting the customer as a vehicle towards inter-agency working

One of the distinct advantages of quality management is its power to transcend boundaries and get people to work outside the boxes. In the commercial sector, even competitors have been known to work together in pursuit of better quality. Quality management creates a practical starting point for shared goals and integrated working practices – providing a common language and starting point for action.

Task

Look at the list of reasons for delighting the customer that have just been outlined. Think through, in relationship to your own service, which of them apply to your service and how important each of them are to its future.

LESSONS FROM THE HISTORY AND PRACTICE OF QUALITY MANAGEMENT

It helps to learn from examples of quality management elsewhere. While quality management is straightforward to explain, it is quite another matter to make it happen well in practice. Some of the mistakes that are often made are set out below.

In many organizations, the process can become too inward-looking. Although there is much discussion about the need for delighting the external customer, some organizations have fallen into the trap of consuming vast quantities of staff time and energies on designing intricate quality procedures and endless efforts to ensure that internal departments are aligned effectively with each other. The external customer or stakeholder hardly gets a look in.

Good quality management begins and ends with the 'voice of the external customer'. While quality standards, procedures and good internal customer/supplier relationships are important ingredients – they are not the place to start. It is vital to begin with the user of the service as the most immediate 'customer'.

In some organizations there is inadequate investment in the foundations for success – both in design and implementation. Insufficient time is taken to plan how best to start, where to start and with whom. Moreover, the staff involved are exhorted to provide a quality service, employ lots of new quality tools and techniques and become enlightened masters of the art of customer care without adequate training, facilities or time. There must be careful prioritization of where to start and then the progressive, incremental and supported roll out of the principles and practices of quality management.

Another common feature of unsuccessful quality strategies is fragmented and inconsistent policy- and decision-making. Although there is often a lot of rhetoric about 'people being our most important asset' and 'quality is all we are in business to do', there is often a vast set of accumulated policies, strategies, procedures, protocols and initiatives which are at best uncoordinated and at worst in opposition to each other. When these polices are then mixed with the raft of implicit 'accepted' practices on promotion, member involvement and strategy formation, the eventual result can be a confusing fragmented mush within which no quality strategy has a hope of succeeding.

Without a doubt, one of the most powerful inhibitors of developing and then implementing an effective quality strategy is insufficient commitment and 'role modelling' from senior leaders, which includes senior officers, elected members, middle managers and trade union officials. Quality management requires a commitment to continuous improvement and front-line empowerment. These principles, in turn, require leaders to be committed to, and capable of, reflection, learning and change; a willingness to share power and authority where it is in the interests of the local community and to challenge management styles based upon bullying, or lack of respect. These are major challenges, but the lessons are clear – superlative performance only comes from organizations where managers and leaders are actively pursuing the principles of continuous improvement.

When attempts are made to change the culture of organizations, a great deal of resource is invested in communicating the message, training people in new skills, introducing new procedures to support the activity and so forth. However, past experience tells us that progress will not be made unless critical restraining factors are dealt with. In every organization there are factors within the structure, the culture or the procedures and practices which are working in the opposite direction of quality management. These restraining factors need to be identified and removed so that progress can be made.

When councils, other public agencies and indeed many organizations embark on a quality management strategy, the initial focus for the efforts may well be on achieving an award (such as 'Investors in People') or developing an approach that is moulded around an 'off-the-shelf' model such as business process re-engineering, or the European Foundation for Quality Management (EFQM) 'Excellence Model'®. Such approaches can lead to 'Fad Fatigue' among the staff (who have 'seen it all before' etc) or engender 'Awardmania'/ 'Model Myopia' so that the models/awards/techniques become the ends not the means, the goals rather than the vehicle for getting there.

There is always the potential for staff cynicism. If this is unchannelled, unexplored or not confronted, seasoned practitioners can be left feeling devalued and angry. Quality management strategists can adopt a 'matador' tactic and gradually wear the 'bulls' down since the strategists have corporate swords and walls to hide behind. However, it is questionable in this contest as to whether anyone actually wins and whether the resource would be better spent harnessing the energy and commitment of the cynics. Any hint of 'Year Zero' thinking should be avoided at all costs; it is always the case that an organization's history has much good practice and many events from which to learn. Presenting quality management, or best value or community engagement as brand new and a break from the past, will not help build for the future.

After all, it is in organizations which demonstrate an unwillingness to learn from the past that the most mistakes are made and the least progress with quality management achieved.

Developing a process for the integration of customer care and community engagement

Good practice suggests that there are some essential ingredients which need to be included in any plan to develop an integrated customer care and community engagement process. Any work to explore customer views of services must be linked to the wider goals of the authority. What counts as an excellent service cannot be considered in a vacuum. Once users and stakeholders have been engaged in defining what services are supposed to achieve, then it is possible to do more detailed work at the service level with staff and users to find out how best to do this. Different customers may want different sorts of service, and overall corporate decisions about outcomes will help to steer a path through the choices available.

Political and managerial leaders need to engage actively in challenging and being challenged to develop skills and attitudes consistent with councils' goals. In this way all stakeholders can be offered an inspiring and unequivocal vision of what the council is seeking to achieve for its community. Ways must be found whereby the leaders (both officers and members) are brought into increasingly close contact with their stakeholders to enable all to learn from each other.

Customer care or quality management needs to be linked into the mainstream management frameworks and corporate strategy. It is obvious that it is frustrating and wasteful to run different processes simultaneously, for example best value, scrutiny panels, service reviews, action zones or partnership activities, investors in people, re-engineering and so forth. There needs to be an overarching and integrating plan which synthesizes the key management priorities – and links together all the council's fundamental performance reviews, cross-cutting strategies and other key plans – which, in turn, must be connected to an integrated and multi-agency community engagement strategy. The purpose of such a strategy is to ensure that all the local public agencies (health, police etc) work together to make the most effective use of their combined resources to involve and engage the local public in the development of a better locality.

The leadership of the change process need to ensure that there are clear and agreed definitions of key terms: best value, quality, stakeholders, engagement and so forth. Without clarity on these terms, there is every chance of uncoordinated action leading to a reduction in the successes achieved.

Case study: Kennet District Council organizational improvement through team development

In 1994, Kennet began a process called 'team development' or 'Teamswork' aimed at improving the management and organizational structure of the Council. Within this broad restructuring agenda, Teamswork has four guiding aims: first, to improve the efficiency of service delivery; second, to improve the effectiveness of services; third, to increase the level of cross-functional working and co-ordination of services; and fourth, to allow a natural reduction in the layers of management to occur through the creation of effective service delivery units. In order to guide the process of change Kennet drew up a team development model. The purpose of this model was several-fold. First, it placed the development of teams on a clear time-scale which allowed the council to chart the development of teams on a two-year scale, depending on how far down the line of restructuring they already were. Second, it helped chart a process in which both team members and their respective team leaders developed their skills and improved the service delivery of their team.

For example, in the case of team leaders, they are expected to move from 'traditional group leadership' to 'Super-leadership', within a two-year period. Although originally developed in 1994, Teamswork has also contributed significantly to the more recent policy framework of best value. According to former Kennet Chief Executive, Mr P Owens:

If one takes the 4C's [of Best Value] Challenge, Compare, Consult and Compete I am fairly confident that the Teamswork programme, coupled with previously established performance management culture, has made it easier for us as an organization to embrace the concept of comparing ourselves to others, bench-marking and moving down the road the consultation.

This statement is backed up by a recent report by the Audit Commission which claims that Kennet performed much higher than average on most of the criteria used for assessing the progress of local authorities in achieving best value. In addition to improving its status in relation to best value, Kennet's Teamswork programme is also viewed to have contributed significantly to the wider improvement of council services. Last year Kennet was acknowledged as one of the most efficient district councils in England; it was placed second in the country for efficiency and quality in answering incoming telephone calls; and was acknowledged as having one of the best housing authorities in the region.

There needs to be the right structure and resources to plan, manage and monitor the process of developing quality and delighting the stakeholders. Typically, organizations that employ quality management principles give the responsibility for co-ordinating efforts to a senior manager, who reports either directly to the chief executive or to one of the other senior directors. This person will convene a steering group and various working parties to plan the actions to be taken. It is vital that the steering group is an equivalent body to the main executive group and that (in the case of local authorities) a parallel member group is also established. There must, therefore, be the authority for the steering group to make connections at the highest level between strategy and operational performance.

There is a need for trained quality facilitators, whose job it is to enable the disparate parts of the council, to learn how best to employ the principles and practices so that the best results are achieved. These facilitators can form part of the communication mechanisms connecting together the stakeholder requirements, front-line staff, middle managers and the strategic steering group.

Good communication is needed to reinforce quality messages and provide vehicles to exchange information and insights around the organization. To this end, an integrated communication strategy is required to support the overall approach. This needs to include provision to educate the key players in the principles and practices of quality management.

Quality management has a wide range of tools, techniques and systems that are custom-designed to enable organizations to get closer to their stakeholders and deliver services that delight the customer first time. However, some organizations have made the mistake of installing these techniques in unco-ordinated and ultimately costly ways. They have adopted what might be called a 'blunderbuss' approach and fired the tools at the organization in the hope that some might just create a worthwhile result. What is needed is the targeted and shrewdly prioritized use of tools, techniques and systems, so that the maximum gain is achieved with the resources available. This, of course, invokes the need for some wise judgements to be made by the steering group informed by diagnostic data.

A selection of quality management tools and techniques

Service process redesign (SPR) involves the redesign of critical work processes in pursuit of dramatic improvements in performance and service. Its success as a tool for quality improvement rests on the belief that service excellence can only be achieved through a careful analysis and 're-engineering' of the cross functional/horizontal processes that theorganization has but often does not manage. SPR involves challenging assumptions about why a process is carried out in certain ways, and re-examining processes from the perspective of different users and stakeholders. It may involve exploiting the potential of information technology such as shared databases and expert systems. The redesign team may well include managers, users, and other stakeholders.

Quality problem-solving groups (QPSGs) began life as quality circles and now include all forms of work teams (sometimes from one department, sometimes from several) whose chosen task is to solve a service problem. The value of this approach comes from the acknowledgement that thosewho are often best at solving a problem are those who are involved in the operating system that produces the problem. QPSGs are also excellent ways to involve staff and service users together to work jointly on service improvement.

Statistical process control (SPC) is a method by which statistical techniques enable the variation in performance of a process to be better understood, managed and ultimately reduced so as to improve effectiveness and efficiency. SPC can be used to overcome 'knee-jerk' responses to changes in service performance by allowing those involved in the process to know what variations in performance are natural and what variations denote that something 'special' is occurring.

Benchmarking is the search for superior practice that leads to better social results. Benchmarking involves analysis, research, comparison, emulation, innovation and action. Benchmarking comes in various forms which include intra-organization, intra-agency, inter-public agency and inter-organizational (ie comparing with practice in very different organizations) benchmarking.

Quality function deployment (QFD) is a technique that originates from the manufacturing industry that seeks to ensure that the 'voice of the customer' is 'heard' at all stages in the design and development of a new product. Its principles and frameworks (including the 'house of quality') can be used to think through the ways in which a service needs to be reframed or created so that its form better reflects the needs and wishes of users for whom the service exists.

Responsibility charting (RC) is a process designed to sort out who needs to do what in complex processes, where many people are involved in carrying out the tasks involved and signing off on the decisions that need to be made. RC clarifies roles, responsibilities and levels of authority that can lead to processes being not only far more effective and efficient, but also much simpler and easier to operate for the people concerned. In addition, it helps to make accountability and responsibility clear.

There are many other techniques and approaches that are used as part of an overall quality management strategy which include, as would be expected, interventions around organizational structure, performance management, cultural development and leadership – all of which need to complement and support the deployment of any of the techniques mentioned above.

There needs to be a strategy for audit, evaluation and review so that change is driven by evidence. A robust approach to audit and measurement helps to give a very strong message to all the stakeholders – staff especially – that quality and customer service are so important that they will be measured with the same rigour as financial measures and other performance indicators. Since 'what you measure is what you get', then quality measures turn attention towards delivering effective service. Moreover, it is important to be able to assess the relationships between cost and quality, and to be sure that the investment in developing better customer care and quality management achieves a 'return' – not just in terms of enhanced user satisfaction, but in terms of better use of resources.

There are various ways of auditing quality. One method that is becoming increasingly common is the EFQM Excellence Model® (see below). The model can be used to evaluate progress towards becoming an 'excellent organization' and can highlight areas where a council might need to invest extra effort in order to make further progress. Another approach is to measure the 'costs of conformance and non-conformance' using the British Standards Institute framework. There are other methods available and indeed many organizations have developed their own models and assessment protocols. Whatever method is chosen, a robust evaluation process is essential.

Tying all this together, there is a need for a performance management strategy which will help individual members of staff identify what they need to do in support of the overall strategy and receive recognition for the efforts that they are putting in. Without such an integrating strategy, there is always a danger that incongruent actions will be rewarded through promotion (for example) while the efforts of the 'quality Trojans' in developing superlativequality, go unrecognized and unrewarded. Most staff share the goal of meeting customer need, and value performance management when it enables them to carry out their work in more effective and efficient ways.

Finally, in addition to managing performance at the operational level, there needs to be feedback loops which enable staff to identify organizational barriers and systems problems; and a process of communication back to senior management that enables them to understand and take action to tackle the obstacles to change.

The hallmark of the organizations which brim with customer delight, effectiveness and efficiency is empowerment of front-line staff – not simply to devise their own better ways of working for and with customers, but to work alongside their managers to change the organization in ways that make this possible.

Barnsley Metropolitan Borough: quality team working

The quality team working initiative was started by Barnsley Metropolitan Borough in 1992 to act as the flagship strategy in their quality management programme. Designed and co-ordinated by the Council's management development unit, the quality teams' strategy is aimed at reconfiguring the management and organization of service delivery on the ground. It is also designed to contribute to the council's general aims of 'helping Barnsley to focus on and sustain continuous service improvements' and promoting 'a more participative style of management'. The process of the quality teams has been devised by Barnsley in order to create a management and organizational structure which is more closely focused on specific – and in most cases narrower – services sectors. They are also designed to help produce a less hierarchical and bureaucratic working environment where every member of staff can contribute to management strategies. As a result, each quality team is made up of a small number of members, usually between 4 and 8, one of whom acts as a team leader. In order to improve services, each team is given six steps to work through. These are: to identify a problem; analyse the problem, generate potential solutions; plan for the solutions; implement the plans; and evaluate their impact. Quality teams do not, however, work without guidance. They are linked together and organized by a corporate steering group which ensures effective implementation of team policy, provides leadership, monitors team effectiveness, and co-ordinates and networks activities across the organization. So far, the quality teams' strategy has been viewed as a success by Barnsley both in promoting a new and improved management and service structure and in terms of enhancing overall staff development. They have also received, as a complement of their success, LGMB funding to create a video called *Quality teams working in Barnsley,* documenting this initiative.

To summarize, a process for the integration of customer care and community engagement within a local authority requires:

- clear and agreed goals for social, economic and environmental well-being;
- all leaders of the council being actively engaged in being challenged and challenging each other;
- an overarching and integrating plan to drive forward on quality;
- an integrated and multi-agency community engagement strategy;
- clear and agreed definitions of key terms: best value, quality, stakeholders, engagement and so forth;
- a structure and resources to plan, manage and monitor the process;
- an integrated communication and education strategy;
- the targeted use of tools, techniques and systems;
- a strategy for audit, evaluation and review;
- a congruent performance management strategy;
- a feedback loop to identify and tackle the restraining forces;
- cultural change to empower staff.

IMPORTANT LESSONS FOR BEST VALUE

Best value is not just a set of more comprehensive quasi-Compulsory Competitive Tendering (CCT) procedures; it is about providing even better services to local people – identified as those that they need and want – and generating tangible improvements in the local community. This can only be achieved by everyone working for or on behalf of local authorities examining their practice and always searching for more effective and efficient ways of carrying out their role. This applies as much to council employees as it does to elected members, partner agencies and contracted suppliers. This is the relentless challenge of continuous improvement which lies at the heart of a best value culture.

In this respect, best value is all about quality management. The task is to develop a working culture which is:

- focused on community needs and wishes;
- convinced there is always a better way;
- restless in its search for more efficiency;
- genuinely seeing staff as resources to be valued and listened to – not exploited;
- based on decision-making by fact rather than whimsy, rank or tradition;
- convinced of the value of process management – bridging boundaries between professions, departments and agencies;

- deeply respectful of the cultures and traditions of the people and communities being served (as well as the diverse cultures of the local authority staff);
- grabbing every opportunity to celebrate success.

To approach best value as if it were just a series of service review procedures will not work well. Quality management contains many practices, techniques and approaches which can be used to support the best value four C's (challenge, consult, compare and compete). Best value also requires a linking of a service-based drive for continuous improvement, with the wider community engagement and cultural change that is explored elsewhere in this book.

EUROPEAN FOUNDATION FOR QUALITY MANAGEMENT

The EFQM Excellence Model® was developed by the European Foundation for Quality Management to enable organizations, who were well advanced with their total quality process, to assess their progress and plans for the future. The model also provides the vehicle by which organizations can compete for recognition at regional, national and European-wide levels.

The Excellence Model is very popular, not just among local authorities, but across the public services and commercial organizations, as it provides a comprehensive, compelling and accessible vision of an 'excellent' organization. The model has a useful focus on users and continuous service improvement. Best value requires making comparisons and the model is almost custom-built for benchmarking. The model places process management in the centre (literally). Best value will achieve more and more if this process theme is employed in thinking about how to enhance service effectiveness and efficiency. Use of the model will greatly assist in the task of deciding which tranches of local authority services need to be put through the fundamental service reviews. Nevertheless, like all models, it fits only partly into the local authority context, and does not provide all the answers for best value.

All 'off-the-shelf' models have drawbacks. Using the model can easily become the end, rather than the means. Vast resources can be consumed (depending on the method selected) in carrying out complex assessment using the model, when in reality the problems are simple, and well known. When things go wrong, frustrated managers may blame the model rather than reflecting on how it was used.

The EFQM Excellence Model® does not highlight the crucial role of members in setting policies and providing leadership. Its origins in the private sector means that it has not been well adapted to the more complex perspectives of multiple stakeholders and customers in the public sector. The model was created to enable organizations to assess themselves as distinct entities with boundaries around processes and policies. It is not geared to deal with the realities of 'joined-up government'. It is not easy to adapt to the current situation of major service reconfiguration between departments, and between organizations that is currently taking place. Modern public management is shifting further towards a partnership model, involving collaboration and co-production, approaches which are rare in the private sector. (However, the EFQM Excellence Model® has been recently revised and many themes are now addressed, including the importance of partnership, incorporating many stakeholder views in the development of strategy and increased focus on all results including social results.) Given the emphasis on challenge within the best value approach, then any model which is employed should be subject to challenge as well. Often, when organizations get involved with the EFQM Excellence Model® for the first time, energy is concentrated on devising procedures for conducting the assessments and carrying them out. The underpinning philosophy becomes one of incremental improvement rather than radical change or redesign. To be fair, this is not implicit in the model and many organizations have used it to make some radical changes. Whatever approach is used, however, there will be important corporate decisions to be made about the scope and style of best value, about ways of consulting with users and stakeholders and about the interactions of different goals and priorities, which cannot be left to simply 'fall out' of any particular model.

CONCLUSION

Any strategy of successful 'managing with the public' requires attention to processes that will lead to improved service delivery. Quality management needs to be integrated with all actions designed to improve performance, develop best value and engage with local communities. This does not mean an anorak preoccupation with procedures and systems – rather a clear focus by staff at all levels on the needs of the service user, and a recognition of the different relationships needed to ensure that the different needs of diverse stakeholders are met. Quality management has many techniques and lessons that are useful in a public sector context, although it is important to understand the diverse relationships that a local authority has to manage, and not to adopt models uncritically. Best value can be used to rethink services to local communities, and to engage users in a process of continuous improvement. All this can help to build services that measurably contribute to helping individuals to shape and realize their ambitions, hopes and dreams.

6 Building a common vision of the future

Anne Bennett

INTRODUCTION

Vision – the heart of the matter

Engaging the community in creating and developing their vision for how they would like things to be is perhaps the most essential building block for making change happen. Yet it is often something which organizations and groups work towards tentatively, and via a range of other activities with slightly different functions, as described elsewhere in this book. Among the reasons for this caution are:

- a sense that the big picture could be so powerful and daunting that expectations and pressures will be hard to handle;
- a difficulty in understanding how to generate the vision, and then how to use it;
- a relative lack of experience in looking at vision and visioning as part of the way things are done in, for and by communities;
- a range of barriers to be overcome, including resistance to change, short-term cycles of planning and action, preconceptions about the attitudes and positions of different stakeholders, from community groups, to politicians, to business, to officers and professionals.

There may also be a cultural resistance to 'vision' lurking in our systems and in our wider society. Many of the case studies, success stories, fundamental concepts and practices come from other countries. However, in each case there is a natural learning curve to follow and some of the lessons are familiar and useful to share here.

This chapter will focus on the 'hows?' and 'whys?' of approaching the visioning aspect of community engagement, with some basic information on different approaches, some examples of when they have been used and to what effect, and – first – some exploration of the barriers to be overcome as well as the helpful changes that will support you on the way. A vision is about the future, but it can be a lot nearer than you think.

STEP 1: THE VISION THING – WHY DO IT?

Some of the commonest reactions that we hear or have felt in relation to the work of generating and using community vision are as follows:

- Vision sounds airy-fairy. I have to live in the real world...
- ...where other people have the power to change things, not me.
- The public want practical actions today, not fantasies about tomorrow.
- Is this a good use of public money and our time?

The arguments set out in Table 6.1 illustrate some key principles and beliefs which underpin visioning. You can probably add to the lists of 'ifs and buts' yourself. Anyway, it will be an important step to talk them through with a number of key players (within and outside the authority) so that feelings and thoughts are aired. However, this will seldom be enough to persuade the scep-tics. The best way to make the case for visioning is to begin it, and ensure that sufficient support, learning time and attention is given to letting the results speak for themselves.

To coin a phrase, there may be 'nothing so practical as a good vision'. The quality of the result and the care with which it is created are just as significant as they would be if judging the merits of any other form of engagement or activity in the process of managing change.

Table 6.1 Examples of some 'ifs and buts' of visioning

Vision CAN	Vision CAN NOT
■ bring together the wishes, hopes and fears of a community	■ compensate for weak leadership across agencies, and poor management within them – particularly limited communication and motivation skills
■ help all those working within and on behalf of a community to align their efforts with these ideas and preferences	■ resolve all differences and conflicting wants and needs – although it offers a strong way of building consensus and recognition of difference
■ focus energy on what matters and be quite specific about what does not matter	■ be assumed to be static – it is evolving and the process of developing and sharing it must be iterative
■ inspire and motivate people to work on difficult or uncertain areas, to try new things and take considered risks	■ be 'project planned' – by their nature, visions are not susceptible to much of the manager's toolkit, a fact which officers in particular need help to feel comfortable with
■ help a community dialogue to take place on issues which are often seen as 'private' or individual goals yet which depend on wider change taking place	■ be developed within the town hall and then sold to the community, if it is to avoid the failure rate of some 'mission and values' statements of the past
■ provide shared language and images as a useful shorthand and basis for other forms of engagement	
■ provide a sense of the bigger picture which is not threatening, overwhelming or only seen by a select few	
■ in today's terms – visioning by the community can help local authorities to be outward looking, working to the local agenda, and be outcomes focused	
■ successfully locate the initiative, ownership and drive for change out in the community, so that agency's role becomes one of enabling and supporting the community to do things, rather than 'be provided for' or 'done to'	

One of the best expressions of the value of clear, shared and powerful vision is to be found in Marvin Weisbord's *Discovering Common Ground* (Weisbord, 1992) whose models (based on work by Alastair Crombie into the 'new politics of interdependence' in Australia) have been adapted here to illustrate what happens with or without visioning. (Weisbord is also the creator of the future search technique, which will be discussed later.)

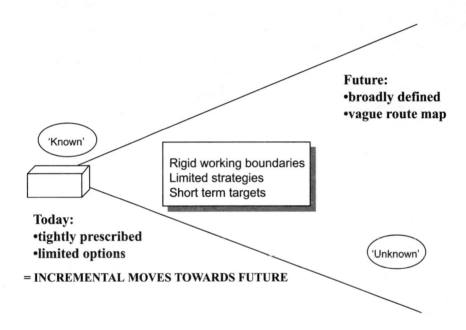

Figure 6.1   Incremental moves towards future

Figure 6.1 shows that if we are overprescriptive on the details of today, and too vague about the direction for tomorrow, then we limit our choices, while at the same time not directing our energies on the longer-term things that really matter. In reality, there are many structures, several strategies and a range of possible goals and objectives which would probably fit with the direction we need to take. In our often task-focused, action-orientated and short-termist organizations, we drive harder on the present-day issues, feeling that those which are further off cannot be worked on today with as much control and visible progress. However, the vaguely stated vision remains unrealized. Several of the more important goals take too long to be reached, and a cycle of fire-fighting and problem-solving self-perpetuates.

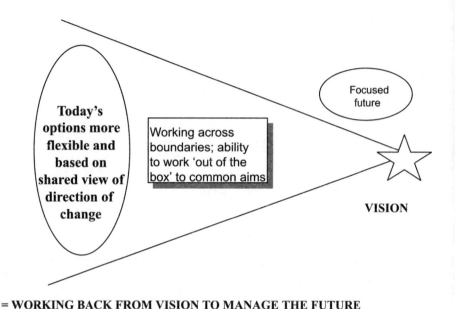

= **WORKING BACK FROM VISION TO MANAGE THE FUTURE**

Figure 6.2   Working back from vision to manage the future

Figure 6.2 shows that when working back from a single and highly refined statement of the vision, the details of how to get there are more readily explored, with less argument as to the one right way to get there, as anything seriously outside the scope of the vision would be easy to spot. More things are possible in the way things are tackled today, and the work of getting to the future vision starts now. The clarity of the vision is held by all those involved in getting there, and so their thoughts and actions are guided by it. Some loosening up of plans and patterns of activity can begin. This is not a far off agenda which is easy to set aside when faced with the distractions and problems of the past and the present. The vision here helps to tie together the past, present and future in a way which strengthens the feeling of making progress over time.

STEP 2: LEARNING ABOUT WHAT WORKS

There are three key elements to appreciate:

1.   the value of the *vision* itself, as a useful product, and its applications;
2.   the importance of the *visioning process* in creating the conditions for success;
3.   the process of *community engagement* as the overarching context.

1. *The vision*   As previously stated, powerful and clear images of the future, expressed in documents, in interactive displays, in art, drama and other media, are the embodiment of much more which is harder to express, point to or measure. Visions are by nature ethereal, but they are also about making a concrete reality. When we can understand something in ways which involve more than words – when we appreciate what the future would be like if we were living in it today – then we have a product which is capable of communicating and engaging with people across many boundaries, and whose applications go well beyond public relations and exhibitions.

2. *The visioning process*   Visioning as a process often forms just part of an exercise, although sometimes it can stand alone. There is an element of visioning in many of the methods described elsewhere in this book, often represented by creative thinking and expression, and looking to the future. Most visioning activity takes place as part of a wider agenda of plans and actions; it should avoid being seen as a one-off, isolated exercise, with no effort to connect back to the present. The process of creating a vision can be individual and personal, but in this context we are concerned with techniques which generate a big picture for the future of a place and its people. In creating a shared vision, people are usually changed by the fact of their participation. Their beliefs and values are respected, but their outlook may be fundamentally changed, along with their sense of capacity to make things happen and to do this as part of a wider community effort, in partnership with others. Thus, the process itself can be designed to be transforming, and many of the ideas are already moving into action without any further input or planning from the authorities or professionals concerned.

3. *Community engagement*   Community engagement and participation is both a means and an end in itself, much as described above. However, the context of local, community-based visioning has been one of the most powerful sources of learning about what works. Private sector experience (as is often the case) gave rise to many of the methods outlined in step 3 below, and it seems odd that the sentiments expressed in large corporations which talk of shared values and vision are often more sincerely and thoroughly developed, and lead to more committed actions than we might more naturally expect from public sector bodies with a duty and constitution based on serving the people. There is plenty of recent evidence that having consensus about what needs to be done does not automatically translate into the desired results, for

example sustainable regeneration projects, environmental strategies, an effective multicultural society, primary care led health care. Many of the 'wicked problems' of today are well understood and are given a great deal of attention through partnerships and projects and policy drives. However, only a few success stories emerge around which much best practice is based. The phenomena of local entrepreneurship and community empowerment are as yet among the least well understood or promoted by mainstream policy-makers and planners. We have at least the rhetoric of consultation and accountability, often from those with little first-hand experience of the power of true engagement. However, as experience spreads, 'the vision thing' is becoming as much a part of the way we do things in local government as the committee cycle has been.

Learning from a history of false starts

Vision is often wrongly associated with such exercises as 'mission and values statements', and so attitudes will have been shaped by the history of success or failure attached to earlier approaches. In some cases local authorities have found their work on producing mission, values, or vision statements to be creative, energizing, dynamic and a boost to any strategy which is firmly based on them. In many other organizations – not just those in the public sector – a number of important lessons need to be learned from what worked and what did not.

1. Ownership through participation

Some mission statements are the product of too few people's input, thus it is the *community engagement* in creating the vision which matters at least as much as the quality and content of the vision itself. In the past only a few leaders and strategists felt capable of articulating their helicopter overviews of the way things were and where they needed to go next. However, aside from whether their vision proved right or wrong, there was a limited chance that these visions were able to actively drive change without commitment and understanding in the hearts and minds of a much wider constituency. Similarly, we should try to put vision on a level above mission. Mission often expresses what it is the core business of an agency or group to achieve. This in itself should be defined in terms of the vision of what the outcomes will look like when the mission is being fulfilled. Finally, the low cost and quick route to drafting mission and values without some process of wider engagement in shaping the words may have only served to confirm what busy and sceptical managers often believed, that is that they make little difference or have limited meaning in day-to-day management terms. We, therefore, need to reframe our approach in many cases so that a fresh understanding of what is in it for all stakeholders can develop.

1. Whole systems and partnerships

The scope of a good vision recognizes the complexity of the real world, and does not fudge the difficult issues. However, by the time it is worked through in a participative way it produces a simple statement or picture which is a more coherent expression of the shared values that will sustain the vision through uncertain times. To achieve this takes broader involvement and more opportunities for joint working to share and develop initially disparate visions. Handled well this need not lead to diluted or compromised versions. Bringing together different perspectives, ideas and information from people across the system (communities, individuals and agencies) allows for new insights to be gained which might otherwise have stayed disconnected. People also have a clearer sense of how the work they intend to do on their piece of the jigsaw fits in with the whole and so can develop this appropriately. New partnerships can form where the mutual interest and interdependence has been realized. Some forms of vision exercises gather up individual visions to share with a wider community. This is a powerful and important dimension which states 'community vision does not supplant personal goals and that individuality counts.

3. Space for creativity

In our world of 'wicked problems' and pressure to solve them, we often overlook the importance of taking a fresh and creative look at the situation. If a vision is too constrained by what people believe to be possible today, then the things they really care about – often not too fantastical – are suppressed. Deliberate efforts are, therefore, needed to encourage people to look beyond what they believe to be today's limitations. Children's participation in such exercises is often the most stimulating and has powerful clarity, as they have few of these inhibitions. However, most adults, whatever their background, have this capacity for creative thinking within them. Several techniques for visioning encourage use of non-verbal media and access feelings and values which go unexpressed in everyday life but which strike at the heart of what drives us on or holds us back. This can even be *fun!* Once we overcome the feeling that this does not feel like 'work', the productivity, innovation and strength of the ideas that follow usually dismiss any doubts about the value of time spent being creative.

4. Local and strategic

In past efforts to be all things to everyone, local authorities may have developed rather bland statements about their role and the aspirations of their district, city or county. From reading many such statements, it soon becomes hard to distinguish one place from another – where are its distinctive features, the unique history, today's specific challenges, the character of the people and place? Members and officers have rightly been concerned to be inclusive and representative, but without stronger input from the community, they often lack the confidence to express the things that add up to a real local identity. The same generalities mean that the vision is of little help when managers and community groups come together to decide what priorities matter, where diverse activities fit together and what to focus on – that is the strategic contribution is limited. Visions can be far more practical than this and allow each stakeholder to interpret their own agenda in a more joined-up way, and then to direct their own efforts in a more strategic (ie purposeful and directed) way.

5. Potential pitfalls

Clearly, some of the misgivings often heard about involving the public apply to the vision dimension. Will it be unrealistic? Is participation real or just tokenistic? Will it lead to frustration or disappointment? Those of you involved in initiating or enabling a visioning process to take place will need to hold on to some key facts:

- it will not be your job to validate or judge the vision;
- the wider the participation, the greater the levels of ownership and shared responsibility for making it happen;
- vision does not mean 'wish-list' – it is not for local authorities to see it as a contract on which they must deliver (otherwise the opportunity to build capacity and empower community action is being lost);
- councils will have the same rights as others to respond to the vision in ways which also recognize other concerns – central government pressures, statutory duties and so on. However, if these are in fierce conflict with local vision, this draws into question how we are defining local governance and the leadership role of elected representatives;
- sustainability is indeed a big challenge – see step 4 below for some pointers on how this process might embed itself in the whole modernization agenda and long-term changes in local government.

STEP 3: HOW TO GO ABOUT IT

This section offers more specific advice about when and how and whether to use different techniques, under three headings:

1. Practical considerations
2. Examples of how it can be done
3. Getting started.

1. Practical considerations

Initiation, planning and sponsoring arrangements

Before embarking on a new exercise, it is usual to have some agreed objectives. By now it will be clear that we need not prescribe what the vision may be like or its potential applications, as these will be discovered later. Some agreement among the initial stakeholders – lead members, community leaders and key partners, perhaps – as to the value and commitment they attach to the work will be vital. This will arise in various ways – from manifesto commitments, amid the modernization strategy, as part of getting into consultation, as part of a larger initiative such as a Social Regeneration Budget (SRB) bid or LA21, or as something for which the time is ripe and support and energy is around. Whoever these key stakeholders are, the key to anchoring the work is not to be too custodial. If the community feels it is joining in with some internal business on behalf of the local authority, then the locus of control is misplaced. An ideal scenario will be to have independent arrangements for steering the project or projects – an arm's length group with a wide cross-section of key stakeholders and community people, with a fair degree of autonomy and support from sponsoring agencies. Budget requirements will vary for different types of exercise. It may be preferable to identify the costs under strategic budget headings to ensure that there is a clear internal association between the visioning work and the core issues for leadership.

What outputs?

Some possible outputs – others are undoubtedly in the process of being created as this area of work lends itself to innovation – are listed below:

- action groups, partnerships, shared interest/initiatives and project start-ups;
- 'map' of area;
- 'map' of issues – showing 'whole picture', illustrating complex joined-up trends/ideas;
- vision fair, exhibition, roadshow; new ways of presenting and gathering in more community responses, sharing and building the vision, interactive displays;
- arts, for example competitions in schools, people's displays, drama;
- video – gives voice to wide cross-section of community, highly accessible and portable;
- data, for example in the form of Post-it clusters, workshop materials, other kinds of records – can be shaped and produced in documents; may be built into a database, for example if gathering in three wishes from individual members of the public, these can be quantified and analysed by categories and groups (age, area of residence etc);
- online dialogues and Web site dissemination.

Some techniques lend themselves to a particular type of output and/or can be designed to generate a range. It will be helpful to anticipate how different outputs might be used and fed into other work, as well as to plan for making use of the content, ideas and learning in other ways within your authority.

How to generate the vision
A sample of some of the best-known and well-used approaches are explained more fully below. Many of these techniques feature as part of an integrated programme within a given event, conference or project which will often include work on identifying contradictions or barriers, shared experiences of the past and present, translation of vision into strategic aims and short-term action plans, review and evaluation processes:

■ Issue a flier or campaign through schools, press, libraries, household leaflet inviting people to *list three wishes or vision statements;* easy to set up, can involve very large numbers of people – lacks the element of getting together with others to share and build joint visions; database can be analysed; preferable to include this data in feedback/further engagement work; costs similar to survey work.

■ Large conference or series of smaller-group events in which groups use techniques such as *brainstorming and prioritization* – requires some facilitation; generates interaction and testing ideas – outputs can be in many formats; costs similar to community conferences or series of focus groups.

■ Large-group event or series of small-group events, in which groups use *guided visualization or inspirited envisioning,* that is techniques in which trained and experienced facilitators stimulate creativity and fresh ideas, and enable people to look beyond current problems (facilitators help people to mentally experience and create their own vision through use of imagination and relaxation, devices like 'a day in your life' in the future etc); logistics and costs as above.

■ *Planning for real* is a well-known approach to involving communities in developing ideas about a geographical area – the visioning element is based on the physical environment, facilities, lifestyles and the needs and wants of people living in the area to be developed. On a model of the area people attach their ideas, comments and reactions using flags or objects – the map evolves over a few weeks with wide participation invited (publicity and accessible location required, plus time and costs in producing the model); one model is used so that ideas can be integrated and processed by those making contributions. Action plans result, and the concrete representation of the community engagement is a lasting output for sustaining and sharing the vision.

■ *Search conferences and other large group interventions* can be designed for a number of purposes (eg organizational redesign, conflict resolution, negotiation and inquiry processes), but 'search' techniques are particularly suited to community/multi-stakeholder engagement and for developing shared ideas about the future on which joint action and consensus may be built. The approach is more structured and expensive than most, usually involves one or more large (up to 100 people) events (of one to three days) and fits with an action-oriented agenda (some examples are outlined below).

■ *Imagine...* is a term, first coined in the USA, encompassing an ongoing process of visioning, taking place through many different projects and initiatives and loosely co-ordinated under a banner heading (for the sake of sharing ideas and news and generating support and sponsorship across sectors and communities). The original ideas are generated through appreciative inquiry (see other chapters) often involving those members of the community who have the greatest stake in the future, for example children, or the socially excluded (some examples are outlined below).

■ *Open simulation* has been developed as a tool to help multiple stakeholders engage in 'learning from the future'. The 1–3-day event is designed to create conditions and features of a planned future which can then be experienced and worked through as if it were now. Participants achieve shared and personal insights about what they do/do not wish to see happen, and ways in which they might expect others to respond. Much of the learning is used by agencies in planning to manage change effectively. There is more scope to develop this approach in ways which focus on creative outputs and community engagement.

■ *Open space* is a phrase which is widely used, but in this context it refers to a technique for working with groups (from 5 to 5000) to enable time, space and motivation to drive the agenda towards shared outputs, be they ideas, action plans, new networks, or write-ups of thoughts in progress. Harrison Owen created the format, which is readily adapted to suit different purposes. With the future as a focus, visioning and shared ideals can be rolled together during an event of 1–3 days while also building capacity and networks on which further development can be based.

■ Participation techniques such as *Act Create Experience* (ACE) and *participatory theatre* are as creative and dramatic as they sound. Highly practical and dynamic in style, they engage small groups in realizing visions, or solutions to problems, or to express thoughts and experiences, both negative and positive, current- and future-based. These approaches can be tremendously powerful sources of ideas and commitment, although they are usually used within specific contexts to engage groups and/or develop themes for wider presentation and consultation work. Specialized facilitation is involved.

■ Many of the consultation techniques described elsewhere in this book have similar characteristics or contain aspects of visioning – such as developing community indicators based on ideal, future standards, or involvement in juries or participatory strategic planning, social audits or action planning groups – each of which sets out to meet an agreed, desirable future. Our focus here is on those methods which are designed to help generate viable visions which bring to life the aspirations of a place and guide and shape all other related activities.

2. Examples of how it can be done

The following are just a few case studies – many more are emerging as local government begins to work on the modernization and best value agendas, with their emphasis on consultation, engagement and achieving outcomes. Sources of further information and ideas can be found in the 'Further reading' section at the end of this book.

Search conferences

The Future Search model created by Marvin Weisbord and associates, and the Search Conference devised by Merrelyn Emery, have been used and refined to work in many different settings, from corporate America to newly forming democracies on the African continent and in aboriginal cultures. In the UK a growing network of practitioners have been facilitating events based on these approaches in public sector and community settings to focus on social outcomes. The key elements are a cross-stakeholder planning group, at least three months' planning time, carefully identified participants (60–100), and a three-day programmed event. During the conference itself, self-managed groups are emphasized; people work in stakeholder and mixed groupings; they explore the past (through timelines on the walls); present (through mind-mapping current trends and evidence and then by relating their own achievements and regrets to this complex reality); and then create visions of the future realized in multi-media and creative ways to express the desired outcomes, achievements and changes. These ideas are then processed by the whole conference into a *common ground* agenda – this is key to Weisbord's approach which emphasizes the degree of shared values and ideals as the best foundation for common action. Action planning then takes place to pursue the agenda in a focused way.

Recent events using this technique include:

■ a three-day event in Newham, east London, 'Common threads', to create a multi-agency and community vision of improved mental health and services. This led to many strategically co-ordinated plans and consultation processes, and an improved sense of connection between service users and professionals;

- a three-day event in Watford 'Fear less in Watford', to create a vision of a safer community as part of the process of developing the crime and community safety strategy for the borough. Key themes included integration and inclusion, and valuing diversity, as well as creating shared responsibility and hope for the future;
- a three-day event in Tynedale, Northumberland, 'Living well in Tynedale, 2010', to create a vision of a healthy life in the area in the future, including all aspects of community activity and regeneration. The challenges of meeting rural and village needs were tackled creatively with themes of joining up resources and empowerment;
- a one-day event in Islington, north London, 'Modernizing Islington', designed to initiate the community planning process for modernizing the borough, and engaging about 90 local stakeholders and residents in visioning the future appearance and ways of living and working in Islington that they would value – key themes emerged around transport, environment and accessible services. The outputs of the event were recorded on video and photographs, and the materials generated by groups were added to make an early exhibition in the community museum where further community engagement will be encouraged.

As a guide, these techniques should not be used where too few people are to be involved or the group lacks diversity. There is no place for formal speeches or spectators – to be there is to be actively involved. Conflicts and problem-solving are not the focus, as these undermine the areas of common ground and potential for shared values across such barriers.

Imagine...

The *Imagine Chicago* movement grew from appreciative inquiry techniques used by schoolchildren (whose stake in the future of the city was high). This involved interviewing civic and business and community leaders to gather their views and values and to challenge them to think about a better future and the part they could be playing to help bring it about. The movement has developed into many more community projects aimed at fulfilling the vision which the schoolchildren imagined.

Projects include: the *Urban Imagination Network* – aiming to improve literacy standards; *Making Civic Connections* using inter-generational conversations and dramatic presentations to help join up the history with the so-called 'newcomer communities', ethnic and religious groups; *Citizen Leaders* which is designed to increase the leadership capacity of residents in at-risk communities and to enable them to organize projects that meet the needs of their communities as they perceive them. This latter initiative trains residents and sponsoring organizations to prepare proposals, organize and implement imaginative community development projects and evaluate and sustain their impact.

The banner 'Imagine...' organization is a small independent co-ordinating body which enables networking and access to resources. Similar initiatives are now being considered for London (and within individual boroughs). Similar techniques were used recently by Blyth Valley District Council to involve schoolchildren in working with key agencies and community leaders to share and develop a view of the future, as a part of the community planning process. A charity called *Projects in Partnership* has used the model (along with many other forms of participative techniques) to help with visioning work in Gloucester and Bristol. A predominant theme in much of their work is sustainability and local agenda 21.

Community discovery

Among the many examples cited in other chapters, the community discovery process for working with large groups of local people is particularly useful for visioning purposes. By asking the participants (50–100) to focus on outcomes rather than today's services and problem areas, they are able to free up their ideas about what future arrangements might look like. They are also able to draw connections across traditional barriers between communities, age groups, services, agencies and problems, to find joined-up ideas and cross-cutting themes.

This approach was recently used in the London Borough of Lewisham as part of a broad strategy of community engagement. Similar events have taken place in Watford and Camden to focus on the desired outcomes for older people and the need for joined-up services and innovation in the approaches taken, the role of carers, and building up neighbourly services through volunteers.

The people's vision

A particularly large-scale example of individual participation in a wide survey of visions was conducted in the run up to the People's Summit in May 1998, coinciding with the G8 leaders' summit, in Birmingham. A large-scale leaflet drop was conducted through networks and media inviting individuals to return a card expressing a vision for a sustainable environment. By tying this in with a high-profile event, the results became part of a dynamic occasion, including a human chain, reported as the largest community action since the Free Mandela campaign and Live Aid. The events were arranged by the Jubilee 2000 Campaign and the New Economics Foundation, whose centre for community visions is co-ordinated by Perry Walker, a well-known practitioner and author on the subject of community participation.

Closer to home, there is a lot of activity within the local government world which is hoping to launch a people's vision for community governance in 2020. This should be a powerful force to add to the vision of modernization which so far is trickling down the usual channels and will need as much participation and local ownership as any local vision if it is to be realized (see below).

3. Getting started

Creating the right approach within the local community will depend on local history, past experiences and current momentum. If building on previous successes, find ways of 'branding' the visioning work and use this to launch some of the less expected approaches in a 'safe' way. However, who has defined the success of previous work? How inclusive and innovative has it been? There is more often a case for making a fresh break from past exercises, to allow for new people to be involved and avoid some people becoming the 'in group' where this might create barriers. Some of the best ways in are the broad surveys and public access approaches. These can then build towards events which can be seen as turning points, with a new identity and a fresh input of commitment and energy for making things happen.

It is the job of today's managers and leaders who are working to achieve outcomes for local communities to develop the visioning level of engagement, as much as to operate through day-to-day problem-solving and cycles of planning. For the best, most sustainable results, look to integrate efforts with corporate priorities and seek sponsorship, commitment and – ideally – direct involvement from key leadership figures in the area. Some resistance to taking part in 'local' events has been seen among those who lead organizations with a wide remit or larger geographical areas. However, the reality is that their large roles are made up of what goes on in these identifiable communities. The risks are that little or no change takes place where this distancing from local action occurs.

The most energizing and supportive role for officers and others engaged in launching the visioning process – whether as part of a wider strategy or for other reasons – comes from networking with others who are actively involved. This form of work undoubtedly creates a generosity of spirit and refreshing openness and sharing across many boundaries. Practitioners and facilitators are usually enthusiasts who are committed to creating events that work on your terms and can help you to assess risk. Ultimately, they aim to share the expertise and build the capacity within agencies and in communities themselves to DIY the work. Therefore, there are a growing number of experienced individuals working within local government who will happily network and share the learning. Finally, the *Democracy Network* is one example of a newer initiative from the Local Government Association, set up to focus on involving people in local government and to support the efforts of authorities who are developing their ideas and practice in this area.

STEP 4: SUSTAINING THE VISION

Today's context – the place of visioning in the modernization agenda
There is a clear vision within the modernization agenda for local government

itself. It is one of fundamental challenge along with the highest of goals. The agenda includes a radical and critical look at why local government exists, what difference it makes to the lives of people in local communities, and how the values of democracy and public service are proved in practice. It also offers the clearest opportunity to demonstrate why there is need for local governance aimed at achieving real change for communities with real needs, hopes and fears.

As such, our most immediate case study into the 'vision thing' is this new agenda. Who owns it? Who would argue with it? Perhaps beleaguered public servants look for the threats behind the promises; maybe politicians look for the opportunity to make voteworthy differences, but the public's expectations are harder to quantify or typify. The policy agenda tells us the public's expectations are generally low (as is election turnout) and the people are in need of local government which will not fail them in the future.

Current policies are saying what committed public service people have wanted to hear – a sense of the value of working for communities; a wish to provide best value; meet need; and achieve positive social outcomes such as social inclusion and community regeneration. We already know, however, that the simple statement of this vision is not sufficient to bring about the change in attitude, pace of change and tangible results that we are aiming at. But how *does* the vision help in the process?

1. Empower yourself if you are to empower others

If we are to make a good job of supporting community efforts at visioning, it is important to appraise the values, motives and attitudes within our own organizations. There is often a mismatch which could undermine the intent of the vision.

There is a conundrum for public servants at the heart of understanding the 'vision thing'. Although we have apparently signed up to working towards a notion of public good by becoming local government or community workers, in fact to spend time and resources on articulating and sharing our personal commitments and motivations seems to be at least an extravagance, and at worst to risk exposure to conflict, ridicule or hopelessness.

In terms of the centre/local partnership across government, the history is one of non-negotiable politics and policy programmes with a lifecycle of their own. At the same time as we see these paradoxical relationships between cautious planners, the expectations of politicians and the performance outcomes as currently measured, we are also becoming ever more sophisticated in our ability to decipher 'spin'.

A more implicit process takes place in public sector bodies, in which professional detachment and neutrality is required in relation to policy goals; bland management statements of good intent are used to preface more pragmatic objective setting; these objectives are based on predictable shorter-term futures which, in turn, fulfil our expectations that the past will dictate the future and we have little power to make it otherwise.

2. Current drivers

The evidence in support of effort spent on visioning is harder to find than with other aspects of practice in public services, perhaps because of its less-tried nature or the difficulty of capturing the essence of it through conventional research methods. However, might not lack of vision perhaps signal one of the key reasons why some so-called wicked problems are never resolved? Fresh and vigorous attacks on important social goals, such as tackling social exclusion, give rise to all too familiar conclusions. For example, among the early findings and subsequent actions planned by the government's Social Exclusion Unit we find a number of clues:

- this will be a long-term process – efforts will be made to facilitate and sustain developments and build capacity over 10 years;
- much of the know-how is out there – all we have to do is share it, taking care to select the evidence-based best practices and transfer learning appropriately;
- efforts need to be more 'joined up' – real partnerships are thin on the ground, and much waste and complacency, unclear accountability and fragmented activity stops 'simple solutions' being put into place – new arrangements and accountable manager posts will be created to oversee a pulling together of the act;
- less credence is given to the idea that – within the spectacular local success stories from which case studies and best practice are drawn – the empowerment and drive are self-created and the ingenuity and entrepreneurialism arise from an inspiring *local* shared vision and values, not merely from methodical application of common sense.

It may be the lack of direct personal experience, political or cultural resistance or the limited vocabulary we have to express such things, but the vision side is under-explored, even at such a critical moment in the modernization agenda. Putting aside for the moment the impatient tone of those charged with getting high-profile results, and their exasperation at what seem to be obvious and surmountable issues which regularly go unresolved, where else does the drive come from to make these changes? What motivations and opportunities exist within communities and within the agencies who work on their behalf? Similarly, what does stand in the way, if we believe that all public servants have some stake in delivering public good, and all communities want these self-evidently positive results?

Using the vision – integration and change management
One possible solution is to mirror the work planned for communities within the stakeholder organizations – with the people on the other side of the boundary. Where possible, directly involve local officers in the same processes, and/or create opportunities to develop a shared vision for the organization which is not subordinate to the community vision, nor corporately detached from it.

The more sustainable visioning processes are those which have developed the 'system', and helped people to identify their connectedness to a wider whole. This leads to more possibilities for self-organizing activity, which agencies should anticipate and encourage as far as possible. It is very easy to regress into caution and avoid risk by taking back some responsibility – a supportive and focused change management group can help to test these assumptions and assess the scope for 'letting go'. If this is not an explicit policy or value within the organization, tensions will be created through some of the approaches used in visioning. It is tempting to set limits around the exercises at the outset but this will almost certainly reduce the value of the outputs and risk uneconomical use of resources in the process.

It is also easy to underestimate the significance of developing relationships. Encouraging networks, communications, joint activities and opportunities to keep people in touch with each other will help increase the chances of ideas turning into action and finding their moment and their champions.

It is normal to see the 'sponsors' or hosts of a large-scale event or project offering to produce a write-up of outputs. Participants will usually concur. However, it is wise to make this an inclusive task in itself, with input from non-sponsor participants, so that ideas are not dulled by being reproduced through a polished communications process. Outputs should aim to reflect the style, tone and something of the process involved at the time.

For large events, in particular, it is helpful to offer to maintain a network of contacts, at least initially – though the database can be shared and transferred to others if they are ready to do this. Also, reunion events and follow-up meetings can be planned, but should avoid being used as a convenient date to return to the theme without any spontaneous action taking place in the meantime, leading to slow progress and little to report back on.

Within the public sector today, one of the most precious resources is the bold leader – whether chief executive, lead member or mayor, a visionary agency chief or maverick entrepreneur within the community or business sector. When one or more of these people are involved in your visioning work, make sure you feel the benefit – public statements, commitments to act, spend money, take a lead and drive the vision forward are invaluable. Sadly, too often the opportunity is missed, either through the lack of individual vision or not seeing a direct responsibility and involvement between their role and the wishes of the community they serve.

However, we should not confuse sustainability with stability. If we are reverting to institutionalizing our community action groups or partnership arrangements, they can quickly ossify, become 'expert', lose legitimacy or risk outliving their sense of purpose. The energy required to sustain a moving, dynamic, often spontaneous agenda of activity is considerable and should be drawn in from all quarters rather than deposited on too few individuals with too limited resources.

7 Working with local councillors

Sue Goss

INTRODUCTION

Local government is not simply a vehicle for service delivery; it is a crucial part of our democratic system. That makes issues of public involvement inevitably complex, since as well as a process of engaging users and potential beneficiaries in thinking about service, we are always also engaging citizens and electors in thinking about the role of the council, and the best ways to spend taxpayers' money.

Local councillors are democratically elected to represent local people, so how do managers get involved in consulting local people without cutting across the role of politicians? If managers fail to ask or answer this question, and develop a participation strategy without the full knowledge and understanding of elected members, they are likely to experience a real political backlash. Members, with some justification, may see their own method of relating to the public – through direct elections, local and community representation and direct surgeries – as having a competitor in terms of the managers' own participation strategy. This is a dangerous position for managers to find themselves in. Managing the boundaries between political and managerial action, and creating complementary and mutually reinforcing processes, is part of the job of managing with the public.

In this chapter, therefore, we examine some of the issues that are important in relation to local democracy; to think about the implications for local government and local councillors, and some of the implications for the process of effective management with the public.

POLITICS AND PUBLIC CONSULTATION

Many of the problems experienced by local councils trying to engage their communities emerge at the interface between the political process and public consultation. There is plenty of scope for things to go wrong. Decisions reached by community workshops or by citizens' juries can be overthrown by politicians with other priorities. Councillors can feel uncomfortable about surveys or polls that seem to judge their performance, and believe that the questions were wrong, or the surveys unrepresentative. Research in the past to explore what communities really think has sometimes been ignored. Radical approaches to user consultation can present politicians with uncomfortable realities, or with the anger or apathy of sections of the population that are usually not heard. In some communities, politicians have lost touch with sections of the community. In many authorities there are virtually no councillors at all under 40 years of age, and links with young people are dangerously weak. Women and people from the ethnic minorities remain under-represented (even more so within top management teams).

On the other hand, politicians, fiercely aware of the financial and policy constraints within which they work, fear that consultation will raise unrealistic expectations, and add to public demands that they cannot meet. They are often frustrated by what they see as badly planned or poorly executed consultation that costs a lot but adds nothing to real knowledge. They are forced to balance a whole series of competing demands, and conflicting priorities. As elected representatives, they have to navigate a narrow course between their party mandate, government requirements, local majoritarian views, and the wide range of different community priorities and choices. Ultimately, it is their success in balancing and judging between competing interests for which they are held to account by the public.

 Task

Think about a recent attempt in your local authority to consult the public. Were councillors involved in thinking it through? Were the different methods discussed with them and were they directly informed of the outcomes and how it related to their strategic work?

In order for consultation to be effective, it must be designed and planned in ways that recognize and respond to political sensitivities, without reinforcing traditional assumptions and prejudices. Good consultation can give councillors better information with which to make decisions, strengthens the information they need in their scrutiny and performance management roles and offers better evidence about the range of views, perceptions and lifestyle choices of the people they represent. Good consultation offers vital support to the democratic process; done badly it simply wastes time and resources, and adds to public cynicism and frustration.

Community planning and public consultation processes can never be 'politics-free'. However, this is not simply because of the presence of elected politicians. Other stakeholders, such as private companies, other public agencies, powerful voluntary organizations and pressure groups have their own agendas, and use their power to secure their own priorities. Without an explicit acceptance of the use, organization, and inequalities of power within a locality, we are likely to carry a very unrealistic view of public engagement. It is often helpful to make the interests of all the key parties as open and transparent as possible – to map out the boundaries and 'no-go' areas, and negotiate within the real decision-making space – rather than pretending that there is a blank sheet of paper.

THE ROLE OF MANAGERS IN SUPPORTING THE POLITICAL PROCESS

For managers developing consultation processes, it is important not to become mini-politicians, but to nevertheless 'read' accurately the political sensitivities, and to design processes that will secure agreement and support. However, political skill is a very different matter from party political involvement. Political awareness is a vital skill in developing effective user engagement. There are a number of useful rules of thumb that probably apply everywhere (such as never to embark on very sensitive user consultation in the three months before a crucial election!), but it will be important to adapt the processes developed to the local situation. That does not necessarily mean repeating the traditional dull methods of the past. However, it does mean designing processes that can gain political support, ensuring that key councillors are engaged at every stage; thinking creatively about ways to develop new skills and capacities for both managers and councillors; and creating space for reflection and thinking outside the traditional group and committee processes. As consultation throws up new learning and ideas, it is vital that councillors are involved in listening, thinking, exploring and developing consensus, rather than simply presented with a committee report at the end of the process.

The relationship between councillors and officers is not always a healthy one. Councillors, especially back-benchers, often believe that the formal processes they are always engaged in are officer-driven, and that officers do not share information either with each other or with councillors. At the same time, officers often feel constrained by traditional structures that are too rigid, making it hard for them to meet councillors face to face in circumstances where they feel able to give honest opinions and judgements. The very formality of the committee structure makes it hard to engage in good discussions or make useful decisions, and is often intimidating for members of the public.

Lack of understanding between councillors and officers can make things worse. Councillors may not have a strong grasp of how the organization works, and many managers have only a hazy view of how political management works. There is a wide diversity of interests represented within any single council. The very process of politics with a capital 'P' can sometimes be seen by officers to make community engagement difficult, especially when their hope is to build a consensus about what the community needs. A prerequisite for effective community engagement is, therefore, good working relationships between councillors and senior managers, and an agreement about both objectives and ways to achieve them.

We have set out below some of the core activities that require shared understanding between managers and politicians, if user engagement is to succeed:

- setting clear objectives and priorities – developing a shared understanding of why consultation is being undertaken, and what it is intended to achieve;
- sharing knowledge about the problems and obstacles, and working jointly to tackle them;
- developing a shared corporate consultation strategy – with agreement about resource use, target audiences, issues to be addressed, involvement of partners, methods chosen, priorities and so forth;
- clarifying the roles and relationships of councillors and managers in consultation processes including formal arrangements – who chairs meetings, to whom are results fed back to and so forth, and informal arrangements such as how are questions answered, how much information is shared and how are other organizations kept informed?;
- ensuring the organization is well equipped to respond – training, organizational change, ensuring good feedback, rapid response and resulting action.

It helps to be clear about the roles that councillors play in consultation for different purposes. For example, members may want to play a leading role in consultation about the priorities for the council as a whole, but to allow officers to conduct service-based consultation about service delivery.

The messages resulting from consultation can be hard to take for councillors as well as managers. It is important that they are examined critically, but not greeted with defensiveness, or self-justification. They can offer valuable learning that can lead to real improvements in relationships. It is important that councillors reflect on their role within the wider community, think about who they 'usually' listen to, which sections of the community they know best and where the gaps may be. Managers and professionals will also have blind spots. It helps if managers take the time to learn from councillors, including back-benchers, about their perceptions of local opinion – after all they are connected to a wide range of networks, voluntary groups, school governors and so forth and have to keep their ears to the ground. Even if their contacts are partial, they offer valuable insights into local views. It is easier if there is recognition among both officers and members of the strengths and gaps in the political process, in order to jointly plan a strategy to fill those gaps, to identify assumptions that should be tested and to fit existing knowledge into a growing picture of the whole local community.

THE CHANGING ROLE OF COUNCILLORS

Councillor roles are already changing. In 1999, new government legislation required all authorities that still rely on the old committee system to switch to a model of an executive mayor, a separation of an executive from a scrutiny role, or both. The mayor or executive will be more clearly held to account for the policy and performance of the council, while back-bench councillors will have a new role in scrutinizing and challenging council actions. At the same time the government is encouraging the greater use of user consultation, citizens' juries, panels, referenda and so forth (see the White Paper on *Modernising Local Government*).

Many local authorities have already been experimenting for some time with different forms of decision-making, with cabinet or executive models, to replace some committees, and have been stripping out the old committee system, replacing many committees with projects and single-issue problem-solving groups. Performance review structures, or best value processes, will also involve councillors in working outside the conventional committee arrangements. At the same time, many councils have begun to set up strategy conferences, community forums, stakeholder conferences, town meetings, select committees and scrutiny committees, and partnerships and joint ventures, all of which require new ways of working. These experiments will inevitably have implications for the processes of community engagement.

Greater public and user involvement creates the possibility of new roles which would extend the range of councillor activity beyond simply 'executive' and 'scrutiny' functions, and which might change the relationships between councillors, managers and the public.

Case study: London Borough of Lewisham

The London Borough of Lewisham established a select committee to look into future political management structures for the borough, following the White Paper on *Modernising Local Government*. This select committee, made up of councillors, met in public and took evidence from a number of sources. In particular, the Council: (1) undertook a survey of local voluntary and community organizations and the business panel; and (2) commissioned a special one-day conference of the local citizens' panel to establish the local community's views and experiences of the current system, to identify what matters to local people and to arrive at a preferred model for local government structures.

The results of these exercises were reported to the select committee, and panel participants from all age groups (school pupils to pensioners) attended to discuss the issues arising with elected members.

Not all councillors welcome the changes, and many prefer the old committee structures, and will try to sustain as much of the traditional set-up as possible. In reality, however, it will be harder and harder to ignore the changed roles and relationships that are developing. Some councils are embracing new roles, and actively exploring alongside local people new ways of working together.

Case study: London Borough of Newham

In order to help establish a vision for the future of the voluntary sector, the London Borough of Newham set up an 11-strong Commission, of which only four were councillors. The other seven members were individuals from the voluntary sector nationally and in London, and from funding organizations.

The Commission used a variety of different approaches to find out views from across the sector including: a consultation paper with a questionnaire; open meetings with local voluntary and community groups; individual interviews with a cross-section of local organizations; and some telephone interviews with other groups.

Working in a borough with large and diverse black and minority ethnic communities, a fragmented voluntary sector, and a history of some tensions both within the sector and between the sector and the council, the aim of this approach was to identify new ways of working together, to build capacity to develop and deliver appropriate services, and to enhance the participation of communities in local democracy.

Some councils are developing new roles and ways of working that go beyond the simple models of executive and scrutiny, and explore the possibility of integrating scrutiny roles with community representation through area forums, neighbourhood panels and so forth. Indeed, there are a range of new possible roles emerging for councillors – as they begin to grasp the potential of new relationships with the community – that go much further than the changes required by legislation.

While the legislation requires a minimum degree of change, there are more interesting roles emerging which councillors may want to explore (shown in Figure 7.1).

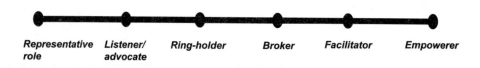

Representative | Listener/ | Ring-holder | Broker | Facilitator | Empowerer
role | advocate

Figure 7.1   New possible roles for councillors

Representative role

The traditional role of the councillor is that of representing the interests of constituents or electors, speaking on their behalf and trying to ensure their interests are carried forward. The representative has been chosen, in part, because of his or her own skills and knowledge to make decisions and choices on behalf of the electorate. The representative role is complicated by the role of 'party representative' selected by a political party to speak to and implement a party programme that has been put to a wider electorate.

Listener/advocate

As communities become more heterogeneous, it becomes harder to 'represent' others simply by taking decisions on their behalf. Councillors increasingly find that they only understand the views of 'people like them' and have to actively find out what their constituents want. This offers an opportunity of a role of listening to the different views and perspectives within the community, and feeding them back to the decision-making processes. In addition, this may involve a role on local forums or committees, a role as a representative on governing bodies of schools or other partnership bodies, attending tenants associations, visiting local ethnic minority groups, church groups, youth groups and so forth, and speaking on behalf of the different sections within the community. A listener advocate may also find that they seek out groups for which they have a particular affinity – environmental groups for example, or organizations for ex-servicemen and women, or for the Asian community, and try to 'speak for' that community of interest within the wider authority.

Ring-holder

The ring-holder role is a strategic or collective role which stems from the recognition of the many different and often conflicting voices within a community. As ring-holder, councillors need to be careful to ensure that all the relevant voices have been heard. The process of finding out who has and has not been heard, and making efforts to redress the balance and fill gaps, is an important part of the role. Once all the voices have been taken into account, the ring-holders make a decision which offers the best balance of satisfaction for the community, and is held to account through the democratic process for the skill and fairness with which they decide.

Broker

The broker role takes the role of a councillor a stage further, so that rather than simply hearing the different voices within a community, the broker will attempt to help the different groups to understand each other, and to negotiate with other agencies and other powerful community 'players' to generate solutions that meet local needs.

Facilitator

The facilitator role may be most important where there are not powerful and well organized-interests, but a relatively fragmented community, perhaps in a rural or deprived area where there are not strong traditions of community representation. The facilitator role is one of creating spaces in which more people can express a view and become involved; helping people to find ways to express what they think, overcoming difficulties of language, knowledge and so forth; creating opportunities for people to hear different views and develop their own thinking and judgements; finding ways to build bridges between people and help them to come to a consensus about future action.

The empowerer

The empowerer role is relatively rare and relates to those situations where there is already a commitment to handing over decision-making to a local community – for example tenants on a local estate making their own decision about whether or not to set up a housing company, or residents in an area earmarked for regeneration deciding how best to spend the available funds. The role here is one of orchestrating the support that the community needs to make decisions well; helping to build capacity by ensuring the right training, information and resources; finding advocates or 'friends' who can support them in navigating through bureaucracy; and creating the right conditions in external agencies to enable their decisions to be carried through into implementation.

Not all councillors will feel comfortable in all these roles and, indeed, it will be perfectly possible for a councillor to choose to stay within one role. Not all these roles will be appropriate in many situations, but we believe that these roles will begin to develop through the new political arrangements alongside the executive and scrutiny roles, particularly as partnership working becomes more common. We argue, however, that it will be helpful within both political and managerial structures to increase the repertoire of roles available, and to widen the awareness of different roles, and the capability to take on different roles when they are appropriate.

Managing relationships with politicians and the public

The role of a manager in working alongside councillors through this process of change is very important. It is not possible to manage working with the public without at the same time finding different sorts of ways to work alongside politicians. The development of a wide range of approaches to user and citizen involvement in the activities of the council requires different ways of working between members and officers.

Until now, interface with members has been concentrated at the directorate and board level of management. Increasingly, middle and junior managers and staff will be working alongside councillors. Managers will have to develop skills not simply in managing their interface with the public, but with their interface with councillors and the space in which they work with both councillors and local people (Figure 7.2). That will require a lot of hard thinking and talking, and honesty and trust in tackling the very real tensions, difficulties and obstacles that may arise.

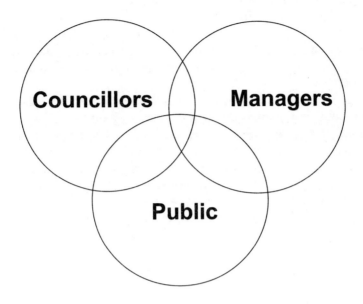

Figure 7.2   The interface between councillors, managers and the public

Councillors may also need managerial support in:

- developing thinking about new roles;
- applying new experimental models;
- developing their own skills – accessing training in negotiation, facilitation, chairing and so forth.

Many councils are developing new forums for an exchange of views between councillors and officers, and for the joint development of capacity; and many of the experiments that will no doubt be explored in other books within this series – project groups, working groups, away-days, joint training sessions and so forth will all offer opportunities to build the right sorts of managerial–political interface to enable effective managing with the public. New approaches to learning including simulations, open-space events, role plays and interactive events will all enable managers and politicians to explore and digest the problems and opportunities that lie ahead.

Managers will need to develop their own roles and skills in response, and will need to change their own ways of working in response. Some of the management of change issues that will be important are explored in Chapter 10. However, there will be some changes that are specifically linked to new ways of working with politicians.

For example, new sorts of working arrangements will require more effective communication skills from managers who will not simply be expected to present a report, but to take part in listening exercises, in dialogue and discussion, in negotiations and in problem-solving groups alongside councillors. Skills in process design, consensus-building and defusing conflict will be important!

Managers and councillors increasingly will work alongside each other in wider forums that also engage the public, such as scrutiny committees, select committees or consensus conferences. Ways of working together will need to be established that enable the forums to be effective. Traditional relationships where officers simply defer to councillors, or offer a range of choices, will not work. Councillors will need sensible, informed advice, guidance about what will work, and help in building relationships.

Managers who represent the council in wider partnerships will want freedom to build agreements and networks, to allocate resources, and to make promises they can keep. Councillors will want to explore new options and possibilities with community representatives without constant constraints from bureaucratic procedures, and will need flexible budgets and responsive delivery systems capable of responding rapidly to user choices.

Increasingly, middle and junior managers will become responsible for managing complex relationships and accountabilities, and will need to develop skills that might previously have been seen as 'senior management skills'. They may spend much more time than before working with councillors, other partner organizations and people within the community. In reality, many middle managers have learnt to juggle competing accountabilities through experience, but they may need considerable support and time to learn to adapt practice and change ways of working to make the most of new opportunities. While middle managers in housing and social services are probably more used to communicating with a wide range of audiences, for managers within environmental services, leisure, libraries and highways – even education – this may be new. It may be important to change channels of communication to ensure that learning by middle managers in touch with the public is transmitted throughout the organization, and that lessons learnt in one department are quickly transferred to others.

Case study: City of Norwich

In Norwich, a simulation of new local community forums involving the voluntary sector, members of the public, councillors and managers highlighted the new and complex roles facing the middle managers assigned to support new local community forums. In the simulation, they quickly experienced a conflict between the need to support the community representatives on the forums, and the need to contribute to the achievement of corporate goals. Through the simulation, they were able to explore how to successfully manage their new roles, and sorts of support and help they needed from senior council managers.

NEGOTIATING ROLES AND BOUNDARIES

Since tensions are likely to emerge at some point between managers and politicians about the boundaries between political and managerial roles, it will be important to negotiate these in advance.

Joint training sessions can be used to explore the different expectations and understandings councillors and senior managers have about each other's roles, and to build mutual understanding about why people do the things they do. These can be used to clear up any potential misunderstandings, and to clarify role descriptions. By using imaginary cases or scenarios, or by conducting 'what if?' exercises, it is possible to identify in advance any problem areas and develop a shared agreement about what should happen if roles overlap or if boundaries are unclear.

It may be helpful to establish agreed protocols or ways of working, but the reality is that there will always be areas where roles work in parallel, or where boundaries are unclear. Politicians cannot make sensible policy decisions without listening to the manager's understanding of what the organization is capable of, and change to the organization is not possible without the leadership of senior managers. At the same time, managers cannot set strategy and organizational goals without access to the political understanding and skill that councillors hold. Any process of community engagement must make use of the links and networks that councillors already have for the benefit of the community.

The building of mutual understanding and respect for the expertise and knowledge that politicians, as well as managers, bring is a vital first step to effective working. By setting in place processes for solving problems when they arise which are honest, open and straight talking, the council will be far more likely to get results.

🖉 Task

Think about your relationship with local councillors. Do they trust you? Do you trust them? What can you do to improve this relationship?

IS DEMOCRACY CHANGING?

We are seeing not simply the evolution of new methods of consultation, but the emergence of new theories and *practices* of what democracy should be like. The reality is that the modern democracies are complex hybrids, involving different levels of representation, complex party politics, different voting and electoral systems, increasing attention to opinion polling and an increasingly powerful media, with increasing opportunities for elements of deliberative and direct democracy. Managers, as well as politicians, will want to keep abreast with the emerging arguments, since they will be playing a role in influencing the outcome.

The view of democracy that has held sway over several hundred years in Britain has been that of representative democracy. We elect individuals every four or five years, both at national and local level, who take decisions about the way that government should act on our behalf. In many ways, representative democracy has served us well, and there are no signs that it is about to change completely. However, there are many changes that have begun to undermine the effectiveness of representative democracy at local level, and indeed it is increasingly being adapted to changing circumstances.

In the first place, the reduction of powers available to local councils over the past 20 years has meant that people no longer have the same sense that they did that 'the council' controlled local affairs. Local councils can no longer control their own finances, set their own level of council tax, raise local business rates, or determine the sorts of service they want to provide in the way they want to provide them. Increasing government control, and the growing number of national standards and indicators, mean that many of the decisions affecting local government are made at national level.

At the same time, it is probably true to say that the public perception of local government inefficiency has been diminished, and that as a result of government action, more people now say that they are satisfied with the quality of local services. The growing proportion of services that are now provided by other agencies, working under contract to local authorities, the reorganization of local government in 1974, the abolition of the GLC and the metropolitan counties, the creation of unitary councils in some areas while two-tier systems survive in others, all help to confuse the public about where power and responsibility lies.

While levels of awareness about councils has remained relatively steady, recent studies have shown that the ability to name service providers has declined sharply, and knowledge declines fast outside the highly educated groups of the community. Respect for local services and local politicians holds up well in comparison with national government. An Economic and Social Research Council (ESRC) study showed that while 92 per cent of interviewees agreed that 'parliament and government waste resources' only 57 per cent believe local councils do. Across the British Attitudes study it is clear that in comparison with MPs, satisfaction with councillors is relatively high. Satisfaction with council services has increased steadily over the past few years (Young and Rao, 1997). Nevertheless, the respect and trust that the public has in government of all sorts has diminished over the past few decades. Voting has dipped sharply, particularly in local elections. Representative democracy has not sustained the interest or the trust of the people.

Changes to representative democracy

It used to be argued that the introduction of party politics distorted representative democracy. For a long time, at local level, the formal processes of decision-making have been designed as if party politics were not in operation, and group meetings and representatives were purely informal arrangements. It is, of course, true that the existence of party manifestos, groups and whips affects the representative role, and individual councillors are often put in a position of having to weigh up party loyalty against the interests of their constituents. On the other hand, the existence of party programmes and strong control by a single party offers the prospect of consistency and sustained strategy through which to guide local government, and makes it possible for the electorate to eject an entire administration and replace it with another one with different political priorities. Nevertheless, the extent to which local elections reflect national trends undermines the view of local elections as a vote of confidence in the local council, and there remain a few 'single party states' where one party has controlled the council since its creation, despite relatively high levels of public dissatisfaction with services. Election reform, particularly the introduction of PR at local level, offer opportunities to strengthen the representativeness of local voting.

We no longer have, if we ever did, a pure representative democracy. Indeed, it is increasingly argued that one of the dimensions of a successful democracy is the existence of a vibrant and energetic civil society, peppered with voluntary organizations, pressure groups, interest groups, self-help organizations and so forth. These voluntary and community groups present their own challenges to elected representatives, but elected politicians at national and local level have increasingly come to terms with the role and value they represent. In addition, many local councils have developed tenants' federations, area committees, carer forums, elderly people's forums and parent–teacher associations, and a wide range of spaces in which the interface between elected councillors and officials meet and work with the voluntary sector.

The introduction of quangos and single-purpose agencies that are not under direct democratic control have complicated the picture of democratic accountability within public services. Many services are provided by organizations that are accountable through committees (eg Registered Social Landlords) or watchdogs (eg community health council, or Ofsted) but are outside the democratic process.

The media has always played a role in mediating between people and government (or thinks it does) and has often formed a focus of protest – a place where dissenting views can be expressed, where alternatives can be put forward and where the wider public can be alerted to the decisions of their elected representatives. This is supported by wide 'voluntary media' newsletters, pressure group leaflets, petitions, presentations, press releases and so forth.

Similarly, the introduction of the opinion poll has meant that national and local politicians no longer simply rely on their own antenna to know what the public want. They increasingly have access to daily information about public views and perspectives. While opinion polling may be less important at local level, most councils now include polling both to understand public views of their own services, and to gauge public opinion over proposed major policy changes. Fishkin (1991) suggests that these changes represent a transition to a 'plebiscitary model' of democracy where representatives act with reference to their perceptions of public opinion.

THE POSSIBILITY OF DIRECT DEMOCRACY

Until recently, the possibility of direct democracy where local people take all the decisions for themselves has always been discounted. There are simply too many of us. However, new technology offers possible solutions. Interactive technology makes it perfectly possible to give all individuals access to constant voting, via the TV, telephone, computer and so forth (Budge, 1996). There is nothing technically preventing the government from offering a stream of decisions to be voted on at the end of, say, the nine o'clock news. The problems are more serious. They relate to the representativeness of the participating group, levels of participation and, far more important, the knowledge base on which people would be deciding. Such a system, it is argued, would, of course, lead to government by prejudice and superstition.

The most powerful argument against direct democracy is that ordinary people do not know much about the decisions they are influencing. The value of professional opinion, built over many years, cannot be discounted, nor the practical knowledge that politicians build up about what will work. Democracy cannot work well unless the decision-makers get a chance to explore the arguments and reach a decision. Fishkin (1991) argues that there are three important preconditions for effective democracy – political equality, so that all voices get an effective hearing; non-tyranny, so that the interests of some potential participants are not destroyed; and deliberation, the exercise of democratic choice in a meaningful way. His solution has been to create deliberative methodologies of community involvement that include elements of direct democracy, but offer an opportunity for ordinary people to explore and discuss, to learn about the complexities of issues and to reach a careful judgement in discussion. The importance of this discussion 'sedate reflection', or 'rich speech' as Fishkin calls it, is explored in practical terms in Chapter 4.

Direct democracy as a contribution to social exclusion

It stands to reason that communities that suffer from multiple deprivation are often left out of conventional political and representational processes. We know that levels of education directly relate to propensity to take part in consultative and government-led activities. We also know that it is far harder for those who live in poverty, suffer ill-health, have young children or disabilities or are elderly to attend meetings. We know that if people are having trouble surviving, they are less likely to lift their heads up to take part in civic affairs. We know that unemployed youngsters are the least likely group in society to want to take part in civic affairs. However, these are the very groups in society that require the greatest levels of attention and support from public services.

The proponents of 'social capital-building' argue that the very creation of the skills of dialogue and discussion, the processes of taking part in local decision-making and influencing local affairs can help to tackle poverty and social exclusion. It stands to reason that people are more likely to suffer from deprivation if they also lack the basic networks of friends and relatives that make life bearable, and if they are isolated and disempowered, it will be harder to gain the confidence and skills necessary to find work. By transferring real decision-making, rather than simply conducting consultation processes, it may be possible to help people build their own skills and capacity. There is some evidence, for example, that housing co-operatives, and tenant-managed estates help to build up people's skills as well as improve the quality of services provided. Community development trusts and regeneration partnerships involve community members on the decision-making board – often elected by local people. Experiments with estate plans, and locality-based community plans begin to extend local decision-making. While local empowerment does not remove the underlying problems of inequality and poverty, it at least begins to redress the imbalance of access to decision-making and control over our own lives.

CONCLUSION

If 'working with the public' is to be effective, managers and politicians are going to have to work together to make it work. We have looked at some of the practical problems and suggested practical approaches to tackling them. Inevitably, however, the role of councillors in public consultation is part of a wider rethink, both of councillor roles, and of the nature of our local democracy. While much of this book has been about the practicalities of current approach to consultation and participation, it is also important for managers and politicians to explore the possibilities of full community empowerment. This has implications for councillors as well as managers, and it will be important to engage both public managers and politicians in a continuing dialogue about the implications of emerging new models, and ways of using the opportunities they create.

8 Empowering the disempowered

Loraine Martins and Clive Miller

INTRODUCTION

In any discussion about community empowerment, there are usually questions raised about how to get through to those groups who do not usually take part in all the regular participative processes, for example disaffected young people, some minority communities, people ground down by poverty, disabled people, mental heath service users and drug misusers. There are often concerns that these groups will be 'hard to reach' or 'hard to talk to'. Behind the questions are a whole range of unspoken assumptions about the capacity and capabilities of such groupings: 'They won't be able to understand what we are talking about'; 'They won't be interested in engaging'; 'They don't know enough to be able to contribute'. In our experience, these fears are superficial. Given enough thought, processes can be built that engage with people from all backgrounds. The real discomfort is probably about what we, as managers and professionals, do not know and do not understand; we have not always found the language and approach that relates well to people who have lives very different from our own. It is the traditional assumptions of a single homogeneous community that is getting in the way, and can make invisible the potential contributions of those on the 'outside'.

There are also subliminal fears about organizational capacity. 'We do not have the skills to respond'; 'Their problems are too big for us to be able to handle'; 'They will make unreasonable demands'; and last but not least there is moral affront: 'Why should we do more for them if they won't even use the opportunities we have already provided'; 'If they choose not to participate that's their problem not ours'. It is these sorts of assumptions that lie behind the failure of many public service organizations to engage with the most marginalized people in their communities. This leads to a cycle of not understanding people's needs, providing services that are ill-suited to meeting them, low take-up and the perpetuation of unmet needs. It is through making marginalized groups more visible and placing greatest need centre stage that public services can begin to engage more with communities, develop the confidence of people so that they choose to participate and take greater ownership of their environment and facilitate the process of empowerment.

 Task

Think about the area that your local authority serves. Reflect on the different groups that live there. Think about those that you 'see' engaging with the council and its services. Who is missing?

SOCIAL EXCLUSION

If as a local authority manager you want community engagement to work it must be designed to meet the needs of the most socially excluded groups in society. Social exclusion debars significant sections of communities from participation. It is also, in itself, the major cause of the large range of problems that concern communities and which most local authority services have been established to tackle. Social exclusion is both a process as well as an outcome. The government's Social Exclusion Unit defines it as an outcome: '… what can happen when individuals or areas suffer from a combination of linked problems such as unemployment, low skills, low incomes, poor housing, high crime environments, bad health and family breakdown and withdrawal from community networks'.

Duffy, for the Council of Europe, defines it in process terms as: 'an inability (of individuals) to participate effectively in economic, social and political and cultural life, alienation and distance from the mainstream society'.

Practically social exclusion means that people:

Socially – become socially isolated, abused or live in fear

They have few friends, family or neighbours that they can call on for help, may be physically or sexually abused, harassed outside the home or live in fear of being burgled or their children getting involved with drugs or crime.

Culturally – are not able to be themselves

They find it hard to get on with their lives because they are put down, or harassed, because of their disability, race, religious beliefs, their social customs, language, food and music or because they are lesbians or gay men.

Economically – cannot afford a decent standard of living

They are unable to afford enough, or good enough quality, housing, food, clothes, heating and the others things that make up a decent standard of living because they are in low-paid or casual jobs, unemployed, living on benefit or the basic state retirement pension.

Politically – cannot get back up

They do not know how to, or cannot get the help they need from politicians, and other decision-makers are not taken seriously by political parties and do not get the backing of powerful pressure groups.

So, you can be socially excluded because you are poor, because you are cut off from other people or are harassed or discriminated against, find it hard to be yourself and cannot get people who can change things to take your problems seriously.

ENGAGEMENT FOR CHANGE

For community engagement to contribute to tackling social exclusion, it must make a difference both to the processes that cause social exclusion and to their outcomes. As a process community engagement should be used to combat social exclusion by bringing people with like concerns together; to combat cultural exclusion by reinforcing and valuing different cultural identities; and to combat political exclusion by enabling people to have a dialogue with key organizations that leads to changes they value. Community engagement should also contribute to outcomes by enabling organizations to understand what it is like to be socially excluded, the causes and how they can be tackled or the impacts of social exclusion alleviated. Working with socially excluded people to produce change is also part of ensuring that whatever changes are made are likely to be effective.

Opening organizations up to community engagement is not a one-shot process. It requires several changes to take place simultaneously in ways of working, in skills, in cultures, communities and in levels of collaboration. As indicated in Figure 8.1, four main changes are required. Organizations need to open themselves up to public engagement. Socially excluded people need to be involved in identifying overall needs and planning the services required to meet them. They also need to be consulted about existing services and how they can be improved. Socially excluded people need help to develop their own community groups and become part of neighbourhood self-help networks, as well as being empowered to be able to approach organizations in ways that get results. As most of the issues that are raised by socially excluded people cannot be tackled by any one organization, public sector organizations must develop effective links with both one another and the private and voluntary sector organizations that are key to meeting the needs of socially excluded people.

Both socially excluded people and staff find that engaging with one another to define issues and produce effective solutions feels very different to the normal service delivery relationship. In the latter, it is the professional who is usually defined as having the knowledge and skills. In the former, the 'socially excluded' become included and develop an equity and validity for their contributions which displaces professional assumptions and adds value to the process of engagement. The power dynamics are equalized and a partnership evolves. Both staff and service users find they need help adjusting to the new relationship – a learning partnership. As a local authority manager, it is this process of change and the tensions in it that you should aim to manage.

Engaging the community encompasses four broad stages which empower groups and individuals and help the public and specifically excluded communities to express their needs and aspirations. Initial interaction should focus on fostering relationships. This has to be undertaken with a sensitivity that encourages people to use their own terminology, language and spheres of reference to express their needs freely.

Once the space for discussing needs, hopes and fears has been created, public services need to be able to reflect both the listening and learning. This will include making some tangible changes. Managers and staff then need to become equipped to change the way they work with communities on a day-to-day basis and find new ways to share and act on community information up, down and across their organization. The simultaneous opening-up of the organization enables marginalized communities to begin to understand the organization and ways in which they can work together. This opening-up to community involvement includes both external consultation processes (surveys, focus groups and deliberative methods) as well as internal changes involving the public in key activities such as staff training and best value reviews.

Public, voluntary and private sector organizations can explore how to work together to maintain links with communities and to meet local communities on their own terms. These new relationships are empowering not only for excluded groups but also for local managers, and can lead to a matrix of part-nerships which are far more responsive to differing needs.

Getting communities and sectors to work together brings a wider range of perspectives, skills, experiences and expertise into the fray and it is the inter-section of these factors that provide opportunities for cross-sector working which strengthens the services and responses to the needs of marginalized communities.

Figure 8.1   Empowering communities

CROSS-SECTOR WORKING

The public sector as a whole and the local authority, in particular, has a way of compartmentalizing people's lives into neat manageable arrangements. However, the human condition does not readily or easily lend itself to separate or individual boxes. Marginalized communities have regularly clam-oured for connected public services because socially excluded groups like any other groupings have multiple needs that cannot be met by any single institution. However, the needs of excluded people are heightened. They require the full

141

range of public services and experience difficulties in accessing private sector services that others can take for granted.

For example, some excluded communities live in areas where there are either no or only high-priced food shops. Additionally, there will either be no banks or they will not have the income to operate a bank account. This can debar them from getting discounts on energy/utilities bills that are available to direct debit customers and lead to them having to pay over the odds to have cheques cashed. Insurance companies discriminate against high-crime areas by either refusing to insure or charging prohibitive premiums. Consequently, if the public sector is to respond effectively to social exclusion, it must not only improve access to its own services but also to those in the private sector.

If the regeneration of a community is a priority, it is possible to build a process that can link engagement with hard-to-reach communities with cross-sector working. For example a management board with a balance of local communities, residents, public services, voluntary and community organizations and private enterprise can work together to assist in the development of sustainable improvements to a locality. Cross-sectoral work of this kind can help the diverse interests to gain a better insight into each other's priorities and thinking, and highlight areas of convergence and collaboration. A board like this also has a responsibility to be mindful of those who are absent, address gaps in its composition and ensure adequate training is provided particularly to those for whom a board structure may be new – building the capacity to participate effectively. As the board grows in its functions and confidence, there will be an increased appreciation of different structures and competing priorities and accountabilities, and ways of working towards consensus where necessary.

 Task

Consider the way in which the service that you are providing lays alongside other services that the local authority is providing. Why has it been organized this way? Does it make access to this service easier or harder for socially excluded people?

Then look at similar services provided by other public sector organizations. Do the different configurations make any sense at all to the consumer, or are they simply ways of making working life easier for service providers?

For example how many people who use the service for the first time would know or care about the difference between the social services and social security? How many would know or care about the difference between housing benefit and other income benefits? Yet, these are not only not delivered by different parts of the organization, but are delivered by very different organizations. For a member of an excluded community, this makes no sense at all and leads them to feel that local and central government do not really know what they are doing. Nevertheless, people are led to believe that the problem is with them and not with government.

COMMUNITY CAPACITY-BUILDING

Our learning shows that community engagement must focus on more than how to structure the dialogue with local people. The first stage of community engagement is to create the space for discussion with local people which is not just a means to an end, but an integral part of the process. If this dialogue and engagement is to deliver outcomes, it must also help people to develop the capacity to help themselves and ensure organizations are geared up to make use of the information they gain to improve services.

Community capacity-building has often been used loosely to refer to any training at local level, including offering basic management skills training to local voluntary organizations. However, if our aim is to reverse the conditions of social exclusion, we must be more precise. Community capacity-building as a process and as an outcome should be aimed at restoring self-respect within communities, and equipping the ordinary members of the community to help themselves and to determine their own outcomes and future. It should actively attempt to create new relationships, friendships and networks within and between communities, to build understanding of the complex issues faced by both agencies and individuals, and create opportunities for local people to take control of the process itself. Effective capacity-building will result in important and significant relationships across sectors and contribute to more active participation in local initiatives and democracy. Capacity-building helps communities to take increased ownership of their environment through devising their own solutions to local problems and working the solutions through with other partners with different approaches.

Bringing people together in such ways helps to rethink, reshape and build fresh relationships which consolidate the social capital that communities bring – the human and physical resources, the history, experience and understanding of the locality and its strengths and weaknesses. This cohesion helps to establish mutual trust and confidence within communities and between communities and agencies. Community capacity-building is the glue that holds relationships together.

CHALLENGING THE 'ACTIVE PROFESSIONAL–PASSIVE CONSUMER' MODEL

Most public service organizations see themselves as providing services to the public which they then consume. The public are usually involved through a process of professional assessment that mostly involves the professional asking questions, drawing conclusions and then deciding what should be done. The role of the service user is, therefore, relatively passive and the assumption is that the professional has the expertise to gain, weigh and interpret the information provided by the user. Although this model of the customer service relationship has been challenged and is changing, it is still not far from being the norm in public services. It is also not confined to the service delivery relationship. Contracts with service providers detail the service provider and client's responsibilities, but seldom (with the exception of tenancy agreements in housing) do they specify what the service user has to do to ensure the service is effective. In local planning, while there has been a great increase in community involvement, local people are still very unlikely to be involved in the design of the community consultation process, the analysis of the information collected or the development of options based on that analysis.

These interactions are underpinned by assumptions about the role and capacity of service users. Service users and/or socially excluded people have things 'done to' them and expectations about their ability and desire to influence the outcomes are limited. Placing service users and socially excluded groups in this position can render them invisible and powerless. The excluded bind their own expectations within a framework which demands little of them yet expects full compliance with existing systems, irrespective of how appropriate or adequate such systems may be.

If people understand that their contribution is simply to be a statistic, they begin to perceive themselves as insignificant and unimportant, or they become cynical and disengaged. Why should they attempt to contribute fully, if the depth of their knowledge is not valued? Socially excluded groups complain that professionals do not listen to the problems and solutions defined by the groups themselves. A system and approach that shifts the relationship from the disengaging process of the 'we know best' to a more equal basis with both professional and service user having vital experience and information is a crucial stage in capacity-building.

The 'active professional –passive consumer' model of thinking does not square with reality either. For example social services departments are seen as protecting children from abuse, or further abuse. They do this by removing 4 per cent of children on the child protection register from their own homes into children's homes or foster care and by enabling the remaining 96 per cent to live more safely with the relevant parts of their family. So, on a day-to-day basis, 96 per cent of children who are seen to be at risk are pro-tected by parts of their families. The social services department certainly plays a key role in ensuring that children are legally protected from further abuse but, within that framework, it is the families that actually do most of the protecting.

In education, it is teachers who structure learning situations but pupils who do the learning. If the pupils refuse to co-operate or parents do not provide them with the support they require, then there is a limit to how far the efforts of even the best teacher can succeed. These examples can be multiplied right across the public sector. In every case, we can see that it is the organization and the service user actively working side by side as co-producers that leads to service effectiveness not the organization 'doing to', or 'for' the consumer. The major problem for community engagement is thus not so much producing a new relationship between organizations and the public, but making the way organizations relate to the public square with the reality of effective co-production.

FROM CONSULTATION TO CO-PRODUCTION

Co-production is a very useful way of conceiving the way organizations cur-rently relate to communities and how this must change if they are to work together more effectively. Figure 8.2 illustrates a range of different levels of engagement between service users and organizations. At one end, we have used the label 'fully serviced' to describe the situation where the organization does everything for the service user and, therefore, all the resources being used come from the organization. At the other end, we have used the label 'unsupported self-help' to describe a situation where the users do everything themselves without any organizational intervention and support. Conse-quently, all the resources supplied come from the community. The majority of public service interventions fall in between these extreme points with differ-ing proportions of resources being supplied by users and organizations. The child protection example, where children remain at home with their families, falls closest to 'supported self-help'; the example of the schoolteacher and pupil 'equal co-production', while local people reporting potholes in the road and persuading the local council to then fill them, is closest to 'uscr-augmcntcd servicing'.

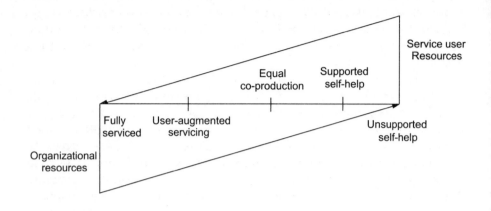

Figure 8.2 How much do service users and organizations
contribute to outcomes?

'Co-production' emphasizes the need to understand the knowledge and skills that service users and their supporters bring to services that make them effective. It is these resources that community capacity-building seeks to enhance and mobilize. This should also become a key part of every service delivery process – the service delivery process should become integral to community engagement. Feedback from community consultation, particularly in the field of social care, shows that the way services are delivered, and in particular the service delivery relationship, often undermines rather than enhances individuals' ability to help themselves. Thus, redesign of service delivery relationships must be expected to be a key outcome of community engagement. Finally, the full potential of community engagement will only be realized once there is a top-to-bottom rethink of the ways in which organizations relate to local communities. This can be illustrated by applying the co-production framework to two examples; one of planning and the other service delivery.

Planning can be broken down into any number of processes – four examples are listed below:

1. designing the planning process;
2. collecting the information;
3. analysing the information;
4. formulating options and deciding which options to pursue.

Figure 8.3 illustrates each of these four tasks across the five-point co-production scale. A continuous line shows the traditional relationship between communities and planners and the dashed line how this is changing with the shift to deliberative methodologies and greater public engagement.

In the traditional model, it is the planners who design the planning process, analyse the information that is collected and formulate the options. The public is involved to some degree in providing information, for example responding to questionnaires or participating in public meetings and in prioritizing, for example by responding to consultation documents. Thus, in the traditional model, the planners control what questions to ask, who to ask and how to do it. They weigh up the information and decide what are the most sensible options to propose. The public has a very small role to play in providing some of the information and commenting on options, but has no real control over the overall agenda. The shifts in planning processes that are now taking place are illustrated by the dashed line. Some organizations are now bringing communities right in at the beginning and working with them on deciding on what issues planning should focus and how the planning process should be structured to enable maximum engagement. The use of deliberative methods has also a far more equal engagement in the collection and analysis of information and the formulation of options. The area which has shown least progress is community involvement in making final decisions on priorities.

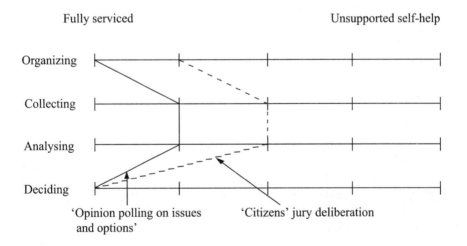

Figure 8.3 Rebalancing the community relationship: planning

The child protection example illustrates how practice can shift at the service delivery level. Where a child is at risk of being abused or has been abused, a conference of all the parties involved is called to share all the available information and to decide how best to ensure the future protection of the child.

Traditionally, this has involved the calling of a child protection case conference. The conference process and the implementation of its decisions can be broken down into four stages: organizing the conference; analysing the information; deciding what should be done; and doing it. Figure 8.4 shows that traditionally the social services department took on the task of organizing the conference. Families would be invited to the conferences but their involvement was highly limited. However, in the case where children stayed with their families, it was the families who took on the majority of the responsibility for implementing the case conference decisions. Both the failure to really involve families and the contradiction between their lack of involvement in decision-making and their great responsibility for implementation led to the development of a new process called a family group conference. This involves the family deciding, jointly with social services, who to invite and taking on the task of ensuring that they turn up at the meeting. The family is then enabled to come up with their own analysis of what the problems are and how they arise. At this stage, social services play the role of facilitator. The decisions about the future care of the child and the need for legal support, in terms of court orders, are decided jointly with social services. In the case of a child returning to its family, the family then takes on the major part of the work of implementing the decisions. This process has been evaluated as not only producing highly effective outcomes but also as being seen as empowering, in its own right, by the families involved.

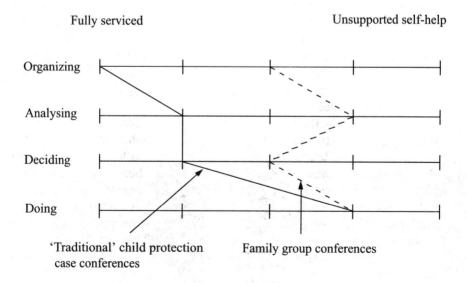

Figure 8.4   Rebalancing the customer relationship: child protection decision-making

WHAT STOPS ENGAGEMENT DELIVERING CHANGE?

Change is unlikely if processes of engagement are 'token' or fail to respond to the problems and barriers facing local people. If consultations are rushed to meet artificial organizational timetables, or funding competition deadlines, this can make real engagement impossible. In the Holly Street project, it took 18 months for the community to build a sense of trust in the authorities, and to acquire the skills to want to take a participative approach forward. Time is not the only problem. Poor venues, where people cannot be heard, bad meeting planning, poor transport, a lack of advance information, vague objectives and restrictive access, all make effective participation impossible. While these problems are well known, and there are very many textbooks and manuals that explain how to overcome them, busy managers still feel so pressured that they are unable to incorporate basic rules of 'best practice'. Sometimes meetings can unwittingly be patronizing or exclusive, and simply serve to reinforce public perceptions of being 'on the outside'. The introduction of problems in organizational terms, a focus on constraints and reasons why things 'cannot be done', defensiveness on the part of professionals, attempts to limit the agenda without prior negotiation and the use of technical papers and jargon, all reinforce the message that real participation is not sought. One eminent doctor ended a presentation to a local community meeting about health needs with a slide on which there was a quotation in Latin!

The process of engagement can flounder because of insufficient investment. Engaging communities and hard-to-reach groups is not a cheap or easy option. Resources will be needed to help facilitate meetings, to develop the skills and capacity of communities, to interpret and translate new developments and initiatives and to hold consultative meetings and focus groups. While establishing and modelling values which place the community and socially excluded groups centre stage costs little, putting the theory into practice requires financial support.

More importantly, there is little point in spending scarce resources to listen to and engage hard-to-reach groups, if there is no political or managerial will to act upon what is learnt. Sometimes, the learning is hard to hear without being defensive, because groups of people who have been excluded are often angry, and can be dismissive of the hard work of managers and professionals. Their views may be uncomfortable, since they may challenge long-held assumptions. However, unless the organization has developed the capacity, in advance to at least take the next step based on what is learnt, the process will simply reinforce community perceptions that 'they never listen', and 'they never change'.

TACKLING THE KEY ISSUES

Self-definition and determination

The process of capacity-building and community engagement needs to enable individuals and groups to identify their own needs and aspirations and in their own words. Focus on developing safe environments in which to explore issues of concern and ways in which communities can articulate their needs to the organization through their own language.

Self-determination involves learning. A dialogue is needed that takes into account both the community's views and the knowledge that professionals can contribute. Care must be taken to avoid the professional information being dominant or having greater value than information provided by communities.

The values of the public sector can be reflected throughout the process of community engagement and at little cost. For example no views should be seen as irrelevant, but this means possessing good facilitative skills to ensure that meetings can stay on course, while some views are recorded to be responded to in other ways. Community meetings may need to be facilitated to help them build skills in determining and defining their own problems and solutions. This may mean the provision of a physical space or a facilitator (eg a community development worker, or an outside facilitator, or a specialist such as a 'tenant's friend'), although it is always important to ensure local people feel in charge of the process, since facilitators can have agendas of their own. Where communities are adequately supported in this process, people are enabled to get more out of their interactions with public managers, and build a greater sense of ownership.

Equity and equality

Groups and communities who will typically be excluded are well known. They should, therefore, be identified and specifically targeted to redress imbalances in resourcing and support. A key to alleviating inequality is ensuring that the work on access meets their specific needs in terms of appropriate staffing, cultural sensitivity and physical location. Local government services need to move the margins of the services and begin to rethink the composition of their communities. The bottom line is that these groups are integral, not apart from, local communities and their views and aspirations and resource needs must be taken seriously. A service that fails a section of the community should be seen as failing in terms of best value as well as in terms of social inclusion. One example is the fire service. The prospect of consulting users has sometimes been seen as irrelevant for the fire service since what we all want from a fire service is 'common sense'. However, findings from one pioneering service showed that the service was failing badly to meet the needs of a section of the Asian community, and that they were disproportionately suffering from the effects of fire.

Access and information

Organizations need to remove the common barriers to involvement such as language, physical access, time of the day, the need for dependant care and payment for time. Consideration of these factors goes a long way to encouraging and enabling more inclusive participation.

Capacity-building needs to be considered not only for communities, but also for the professionals, to support the developing understanding of one another's worlds, ways of thinking, motivations and language. For example where organizations use clear and direct language and appropriate interpreters, there is less room for confusion and misinterpretation and greater clarity of purpose and improved communication.

Communication

Good communication is essential. If work is to be done collaboratively within communities, then it is important that all participants have access to all the information and the means to understand it. For example holding a focus group of young people in a venue that is familiar and welcoming to them, in language which is free of jargon and not patronizing, creates an environment which assists young people to make contributions on their own terms and turf. Organizations can use a variety of approaches to include people who find written information less accessible, such as videos, tapes, methods such as planning for real, simulations and group discussions.

In summary of this chapter, we have listed below in Table 8.1 a checklist of the methods for developing inclusive services.

Table 8.1   Checklist: developing inclusive services

Typical Problem	Action
'Until the government intervened it was possible for water companies to disconnect people who were unable to pay their bills. Now the government requires the companies to provide water as of right'	*Availability* making sure that essential services are available to people or cannot be withdrawn
'A child who is a wheelchair user not being able to join in all the school activities as some parts of the school are not wheelchair accessible'	*Physical access* making sure all parts of buildings and public transport are physically accessible and are easy to use by disabled people with physical or sensory impairment
'Where parents cannot speak English children may often act as interpreters. This can sometimes be very inappropriate, for example, when a child is asked by a doctor to interpret for his mother who is seeking contraceptive advice'	*Language* The provision of staff who speak the service user's language or easily accessible interpreters
'The number of dentists who will take NHS patients is becoming so few that people must now travel long distances to visit one'	*Location* Making the service available in people's homes, or close to where people live or work or next to other facilities that they use frequently
'Having to take time off from work to use services that are only open during working hours either causes hardship through lost wages or puts people off using the service'	*Opening times* Fitting opening times around working hours and when a service is most likely to be needed
'Bullying on the way to or from school, or in school, is a major reason why some children either truant or cannot settle and learn'	*Safety* Ensuring that service users are not harassed, or fear harassment, going to or from a service or when they are using it
'Insurance companies charging extremely high premiums, or refusing to insure people in certain areas, mean that socially excluded people are doubly disadvantaged'	*Eligibility* The removal of rules that mean that an excluded person is not eligible for a service

'Socially excluded people are least likely to have a phone. Using public call boxes is inconvenient and costly, especially when helplines keep people waiting'

Communications
Ensuring that services which are accessed by phone or computer are equally available to people who do not have this equipment in their own homes

'Not providing women-only facilities, and refusing to relax the rules to allow the wearing of certain clothes, in order that some Asian women could make use of a public swimming pool'

Socially acceptable
Taking into account social and religious norms that would otherwise stop someone using a service

'Although discounts are available for a wide range of services, each one requires a separate application to be made. This process is complex, time-consuming and confusing and puts many people off'

Cost
Where a charge is made for a service ensuring that people are not excluded by providing it free or at a reduced cost and with the minimum of bureaucracy

'The provision of a special public display of books and information signposted as being for people who are unemployed'

Non-stigmatizing
Ensuring the way a service is advertised, made available or delivered does not lead the service users to feel stigmatized

Changing the organization to be effective at user engagement

9

Paul Tarplett

'It's difficult to exaggerate the change in thinking that is required of central government and civil servants, away from a top down approach towards one rooted in the needs and skills of local communities.'

(Report of the Commission on Social Justice, 1994)

INTRODUCTION

It is the argument of this book that the public sector both needs and is able to become much more attuned to its users. In this chapter we will look at how this involvement will create very real pressures for organizational change, the direction of that change and how to bring it about.

Most people working in local authorities probably feel that they have had more than enough change already and could be forgiven for not wanting more. Yet, as the above quote suggests, a change in the mindset and culture of public sector organizations and those that work within them is essential. At its most basic, local authorities need to engage successfully with their users and other stakeholders to ensure continued survival. More optimistically, they need to find ways to integrate the many pressures for change and the various initiatives which are being undertaken to improve their performance. However, it is not feasible to keep asking staff to do more with less, to manage further change while delivering high quality services in the here and now, within the current structures and systems of most public sector organizations. We need to find ways of designing organizations which better integrate the delivery of 'the day job' with the demands to respond to external pressures and to create something new for the future. In the private sector, this would be called 'designing' marketing or 'customer-led organizations'. In the public sector, the imperative is to design 'user-led' or 'stakeholder-led' organizations.

Who is this chapter for?

Designing user-led organizations might be seen as the province of the chief executive and the directors and undoubtedly it is more likely to fall within their job descriptions than those of more junior managers. However, there are several reasons why there is a wider responsibility. The nature of user involvement is that the most senior people are usually the furthest removed from it and need to draw upon the experiences of those who are closer. The key to effective change is extracting the learning from past and present experience, therefore creating a climate where all can contribute will be an important role for all managers. Most fundamentally, however, it is possible for any manager to adopt a user-focused mindset and to develop his or her part of the organization to work in this way. We hope that the ideas and techniques suggested in this chapter will be of use to all managers as well as those operating at the director level.

THE PRESSURES FOR ORGANIZATION CHANGE

For some, user involvement may be an end in itself. Others may be persuaded that it is a necessary response to other pressures, such as meeting government requirements. However, even the most reluctant are still likely to face the same external and internal pressures for change, which are outlined below. These point to the need to do something different. User engagement is both a pressure to change and a way of integrating our responses to the many other pressures which exist.

The impact of user perspectives on organizations

The need to change is often obvious the moment services are considered from a user point of view. If they are found to be inadequate, this challenges us to do something different or to do it in a different way. A simple example might be the transportation of elderly people to day centres. The individual pensioner may feel the hours spent on the bus collecting other old people is not worth the time out, but since they are not listened to, they have no choice but to go. The professional view may be a combination of 'it's good for you' and 'we have to manage the service for everyone, not just for you'. However, few of us would tolerate this loss of free will earlier in our lives or in our dealings with the private sector. This well-meaning, but inflexible attitude, led one mental health worker to comment of his profession: 'We're so bloody patronizing, believing we know how people should live and dress'. Once we recognize that our services are not delivering what our users want, the next step is to change them.

Chris Skelcher identifies a series of disempowering actions in service delivery, which themselves provide an agenda for change:

- telling not asking;
- being asked then given something different;
- not being given entitlements/not being treated equitably;
- not being given any choice;
- having to repeat story to different officials with no progress;
- users being kept waiting in ignorance of decisions being made about them.

This mindset has sometimes carried over into the involvement process, in effect disempowering users even though the intention may have been otherwise. Typically, involving such actions as people:

- not being involved in decisions which affect them;
- being invited to devote energy to no apparent effect;
- discovering that the people who offered involvement had already decided what to do;
- wanting to be involved but being excluded while others are included;
- at last being involved and then getting the message in various ways that their group is less important;
- not having the same opportunities to be involved as others;
- not being supported to be involved in the way they want;
- discovering that the parameters of the exercise have changed without being involved in the decision;
- believing that at last here was an official process they could trust and then being let down.

(Skelcher, 1993)

Many of these behaviours and ways of working have been driven by the organizational structures and decision-making processes within which we all work. Staff do not choose to be unhelpful, but if they have no decision- making power themselves, they often feel unable to help. If different parts of the organization are not connected well, members of the public may find themselves shunted from one department to another. If systems are rigid, exceptions cannot be made even when it 'makes sense' for all concerned. If politicians have no way of learning from front-line staff or users, they may make decisions that run counter to changing needs. In the same way, rigid vertical structures or over-bureaucratized systems can fragment the consultation process itself, leading to duplication, failure to learn lessons, and failure to change in response to what is heard. If we are to listen effectively to users, we need to change our organizations.

Involving managers and staff

Even if managers and staff accept that user involvement is desirable in its own right or essential for the organization's survival, they may feel less than enthusiastic about taking on more responsibilities in this direction. All change is unsettling for some staff and previous experiences of user engagement may have been difficult. Becoming more user-focused can be experienced as particularly threatening because it can be seen as giving up some professional power to decide what is done. There are two points to make here. First, staff need to be involved, just as much as service users. Disempowered people cannot empower others. People need to be given a chance to understand the reasons for change, to voice their concerns and as far as possible to influence the nature of the response to users. This should be a continuing process as individuals and organizations learn from their involvement with users. Managers and staff are also stakeholders and while it would be wrong to pretend there is no tension between meeting the needs of users and those of other stakeholders, it is equally clear that the skills and commitment of those who work inside local authorities are essential to making user involvement a success. We know that successful organizations concern themselves with the welfare of their own staff (see, for example, 'Impact of people management practices on business performance', IPD paper no 22) but it is more that that. If organizations are to seek the views of users and involve them in decisions about service delivery, it will be the staff who do so. They must make it work.

This is not to say that staff can have a veto over the direction of change. In the past, staff views and needs have been seen to 'drown out' the views of service users, and local authorities were often seen as 'producer-dominated'. Managers have the difficult task of balancing the user interest against those of other stakeholders such as their staff and the wider tax paying public and their representatives.

Given the difficulty of this balancing act, added to all the real pressures to deliver 'the day job' it would not be surprising if most managers decided not to bother trying to change their organizations and make them more user-focused. It is essential, therefore, that managers are given space and encouragement to experiment and support to learn from and overcome difficulties. The creation of 'new organizations' is, therefore, central to achieving greater user involvement.

Organizational change is multi-dimensional

To understand why, despite good intentions, a shift to a user focus is difficult, it helps to look at all the different dimensions of an organization or delivery system.

There are many frameworks or models to choose from, but typically they share the following dimensions:

- purpose or mission – to answer the question 'What is the organization for?';
- strategy – to determine how the organization will achieve its purpose;
- job and work design – how roles and responsibilities are allocated;
- structure – hierarchical and non-hierarchical working relationships;
- information and decision-making – communication up, down and across the organization and the allocation of authority to take decisions;
- reward systems – what is rewarded and how – behaviours, skills, perceived performance of individuals, teams and whole organization;
- competencies, skills and knowledge to undertake what is required, and the underpinning personnel policies and practices;
- leadership – to articulate the mission and vision and orchestrate the resources of the organization so that these can be achieved;
- culture – the symbols and behaviours which reveal the values of the organization.

All these may need to change. Some, such as mission and strategy, may be already changing to respond to new political and environmental realities. However unless matching changes take place in structures, systems, rewards, capabilities and the other elements of organizational design, it is unlikely that new strategies will be successfully implemented. We know that change in one dimension alone is unlikely to succeed. Often structures are reorganized, but if attention is not paid to culture or motivation, old traditions survive. Effort spent on changing the culture may be wasted if rigid systems or structures undermine new ways of doing things. In addition, if the reward system does not recognize the new goals and strategy then managers will be rewarded for refusing to change.

This is a huge area of debate and study, and in this chapter we can do no more than sketch out the most important issues. Writers such as Charles Handy, Peter Senge and Peter Drucker talk about organizational and culture change, and the new Improvement and Development Agency is building models of good practice for modern local authorities. (We set out ideas for other books on this subject in the 'Further reading' section at the end of this book.) Change in each of the 'dimensions' of an organization is difficult, but perhaps the most difficult area is the interface between capability, culture, and structure. Often these can reinforce each other. If change takes place in only one area, other drivers force the organization back into old ways. However, if culture and structure are addressed at the same time, they have a positive reinforcing effect. We, will therefore, pay particular attention to those, and the broader systems which support them.

CULTURE

By organizational culture, we mean the informal symbols and behaviours that reveal the values of the local authority. They are seldom formalized, but include the unspoken and unwritten 'rules' about how things are done, what is considered important, what sorts of attributes are rewarded, and how people should spend their time.

Some of the strongest 'cultures' come from within the professions that make up local authorities; social work, architecture, housing management, engineering, environmental health, teaching, youth work, librarianship – and many more. Each of these professions may carry powerful assumptions and attitudes that are reinforced through professional work practice and training. These may create barriers to change, since deep-seated professional views about 'how things should be done' are hard to shift.

Individual local authorities may also develop their own organizational or departmental, or even sub-departmental cultures. Often, local authorities seem from the outside to have strong 'personalities' which are not simply reducible to political differences. In one authority, for example, there may be strong values about looking after each other, or caring for staff, which are missing in another. Some local authorities value cleverness, others value practical skills; some value thoroughness while others value speed. In some, strong leadership is taken for granted while in others it is considered suspect.

Culture is also affected by the systemic pressures that occur within public services. In the private sector the potential excess of wants over available resources is choked off by the price mechanism. Rising prices reduce demand to what is available and/or encourages new suppliers to make suitable provision. At the individual level, people can usually obtain the quality and quantity of services they want provided they are willing to pay enough. From an organizational perspective no one has to make an administrative decision about who receives which services or to worry about whether enough is being provided. In the public sector, demand for services which are free at the point of delivery will mean that demand always exceeds supply and, therefore, someone has to make a rationing decision. Such decisions are all the more onerous because they may well involve issues of individual well-being and public welfare. This has pushed professionals into making resource allocation decisions. Given this responsibility, it is relatively easy for professionals to come to believe that they are the only ones who should make such decisions. The absence of pressure to delight customers, and the excess of public needs over what can be resourced, can lead, relatively easily, to a culture where providers of public services believe that they know better than users what should be provided. They may feel justified in a suspicion that each user will claim what they want for themselves, regardless of the needs of others. Managers and staff are held to account for equity, probity and value for money. Building user views into service planning and delivery, therefore, provides a counterbalance to the danger of producer complacency. It provides professionals with vital input into what should be provided at what level and in what manner.

The absence of a price mechanism and the associated profit motive has a further effect on the culture of local authorities. Like their private sector counterparts, they need to satisfy several different stakeholder groups if they are to survive in the long term. However, in the absence of a profit measure, public sector organizations have found it harder to determine what good performance would be and have tended to measure inputs rather than outputs and outcomes. They have experienced particular problems in determining priorities and in satisfying the interests and aspirations of different stakeholders. The absence of a direct link between customer satisfaction and the financial security of public sector organizations has had several effects. It has reduced the pressure to seek efficiency gains; led to a greater concern with inputs rather than outputs or outcomes and made it harder for local authorities to determine priorities and innovate in pursuit of objectives. It has also made them more responsive to the articulate, middle class who tend to receive disproportionate quantity and quality of the limited resources available. Recent research on differential survival rates for cancer sufferers is the latest example of how the better off seem to do better. Well-structured and supported user engagement can provide a powerful lever for change because it affects these systemic pressures. Users can help organizations to determine priorities and offer an important source of feedback on past performance and, therefore, provide pressure for future improvement.

It is important to emphasize here that individuals within the system are not at fault for what they have done or how they have worked. On the contrary, most have tried very hard in difficult circumstances to deliver high quality services. However, pressures within the system have often interacted to create unhelpful cultures and undesirable outcomes. Rather than seeing these as 'someone's fault', it is important to examine how these arrangements can be changed to improve the effectiveness and efficiency of what is provided.

That does not mean under-estimating what is involved. The current structures and systems are a response to pressures that will not go away just because arrangements are changed. It may seem relatively straightforward to change structures and systems but it is far harder to change the informal culture of organizations or professionals. We need to begin to understand the attitudes and beliefs that underpin culture and behaviours and the factors that reinforce them, otherwise change will merely create more confusion.

Change is not all one way. By involving service users, we can change the role they play in the 'culture' – moving from passive (and complaining) consumers to co-producers able to take more responsibility for what happens, to recognize what can and cannot be achieved and to make trade offs. This is harder than blaming others for not making services available. As will be seen below a key aspect of the organizational change required by user engagement is the building of capacity among users to play their role.

Changing structure – challenging departmental "silos"

Opening service providers to the views of users and to their input in areas of service design and delivery will both necessitate and support wider organizational change. Users are generally blind to organizational systems and structures except in the impact they have on what they receive. Their emphasis is likely to be on practical results which impact positively on their lives. This may require managers and staff from different departmental 'silos' to come together and agree their different roles in contributing to these ends. In order to involve and respond to users, organizations will need to rethink structures and systems to organize services in more user-focused ways. Part of this would certainly involve finding ways to give voice to users in decision- making at different stages of the process, from assessment of need through service delivery to evaluation of outcomes.

User engagement needs to be supported by appropriate organizational structures. These need to provide mechanisms for bringing users and providers together, to help staff to listen, balance and make judgements about potentially conflicting needs. They need to provide space for those close to users to respond and make changes, not simply to pass requests up the line. This might involve having the authority to spend sums of money or to create new relationships with other providers. A simple example might be authorizing front-line housing staff to commission minor repairs, within an overall budget. However, it is difficult, if not impossible, to achieve these changes within traditional departmental 'silos' or command and control cultures.

Moving from command and control

The dominant mode of organization design in the UK for most of the 20th century has been based on, what might be termed 'command and control'. This has been true in both the public and private sectors. Using the framework of organization design given earlier, we can see that its main features in the public sector have been:

- purpose – to deliver what services it felt were needed/required by law within the financial constraints set by central government;
- strategy – a mix of broad aspirations and detailed descriptions of what would be provided in future, often bearing little relation to operational reality;
- hierarchical structures, with functional/professional groups as a basis of separate departments;
- tightly defined roles, specialized jobs and, close supervision;
- top-down decision-making, with authority retained at or near the top;
- rewards based on size of resources controlled and accurate implementation of policies and procedures;
- key skills defined in terms of function and technical/professional expertise personnel policies and, rules and regulations designed to maintain tight control of the activities of the workforce;
- culture – rule following, risk averse, absence of initiative and tendency to see putting own interests first as being in best interest of users.

These methods of operation are becoming unsustainable as new work and approaches have been grafted on to old structures and systems, creating tensions and undeliverable workloads. The potential gain from going through the pain of further change, therefore, is the creation of sustainable, healthier workplaces which serve their staff better as well as their users.

Private sector organizations have achieved long-term success through becoming 'marketing-led', that is focused on the needs of groups of consumers while satisfying the demands of other stakeholders. Such companies have had to rethink their organization design because it was clear that it was impossible to meet the rising expectations of customers and the threat from competitors within a command and control framework. As we have seen, similar pressures also apply in the public sector, notably rising public expectations and restricted finance.

The dilemma of how to satisfy these expectations for more and better services, while reducing costs, is not solvable within the framework of command and control within the public sector any more than in the private sector. There are several reasons for this:

- it is expensive – requiring layers of management to determine what is to be done and tell people how to do it;
- it is slow – it takes time for front-line staff to pass requests on to senior colleagues and for replies to come back;
- it is inefficient – several people have to review or hear a story in order to give a decision;
- each management layer diverts others from serving customers by asking for information so that they can manage;
- junior staff become unwilling and possibly unable to make decisions – deskilled as well as disempowered.

Routes to change

The old ways of doing things simply cannot cope with the increasing pressures brought about by greater user and public engagement. However, the very processes that work well at engaging users begin to offer a solution. User engagement can be a lever for change, as well as producing different models which are more effective at coping with the complex world local authorities now face. This changing nature of work is itself a response to the demands of the external environment and requires different types of organizations and different skills and attitudes from the people who work in them.

Many of the new initiatives set up by local authorities in response to the new government agenda are already organized in very different ways. Health and employment action zones, and local initiatives on crime, community safety, youth, employment, and environmental sustainability all focus on outcomes which cannot be achieved through traditional vertical departments. They require partnership/co-operation cutting across boundaries. Many organizations set up horizontal project teams to handle the 'new work'. These do not sit easily with old command and control approaches, that are retained for the delivery of traditional services. However, managers and staff feel increasingly that they are being squeezed between the need to deliver good services now, in their 'day job', within a traditional framework, while taking on a whole new set of responsibilities for change and extra projects. The simultaneous use of two competing organizational arrangements duplicates work, and weakens accountabilities. Ultimately, it is untenable, since there are not enough hours in the day for the existing and new tasks to be done in this way.

The contrast between the old and new ways of organizing are summarized in Table 9.1.

Table 9.1   Contrast between the 'old' and 'new' ways of organizing

Old Way	New Way
Structures departments – deciding which functions will be grouped together	*Structures* horizontal working – mapping out the core organizational process and their co-ordinating mechanisms
Working relationships and authority line management – a focus on the span of control, communication and responsibility for quality improvements	*Working relationships and authority* team-working, upwards and lateral as well as downwards communication; decentralized decision-making
Job descriptions producing individual job descriptions to clarify contributions; rigidity if 'not my job'	*Job descriptions* flexibility of requirements – defining the accountabilities of teams and devising capability/competency frameworks that spell out the performance requirements
Work design (roles/responsibilities) defining work only in terms of function, professional expertise, customer, task, etc	*Work design (roles/responsibilities)* broad responsibility for outputs and outcomes, and for managing customer/task/supplier relationships; doing what is needed to deliver now, while encouraging change and innovation

(Adapted from: Report of the Commission on Social Justice (1994))

The way forward must be to begin to change the ways we design organizations, the ways we see the culture of the organizations, and the capabilities, knowledge and skills we require of managers and staff.

KEY ELEMENTS OF REDESIGNED ORGANIZATIONS

We have already argued that certain principles should underpin organizational design. In summary, these are as follows:

- move from 'the professional knows best' to at least joint decision-making in the overall planning of services and resource allocation;
- building user views into service planning and delivery;
- use feedback from users and other stakeholders as pressure for continuous improvement;

- maintain focus on outputs and outcomes rather than inputs or processes;
- organize user involvement on the basis of their issues not organizational structures;
- keep internal structures and external organizational boundaries flexible and influenced by needs and function;
- recognize that it will not be easy to listen to and involve users, so support front-line staff and managers involved in this;
- move away from tight mechanistic, command and control models of organization design to looser, more dispersed authority and intelligence;
- build learning into the organization by allowing users and other stakeholders to challenge underlying norms of systems and behaviours.

The way in which work is designed, and roles and responsibilities allocated, will be changed considerably in response to an increase in the level of user involvement and the above principles. Work which is currently undertaken inside the organization may be moved outside, for example the passing of information to users may be undertaken by user groups. Work currently undertaken at a senior level may move closer to the front line, for example reviewing performance. The role of more senior staff may be to find ways to enable decisions taken by users and front-line staff to be effective, for example ensuring that they get the management information they need. Work may be designed around outcomes or user issues rather than professional disciplines, for example allowing one professional to undertake an assessment covering the work of different professions.

Changes to work design and roles and responsibilities will be supported by changes in structures, perhaps creating project or combined service groups rather than traditional departments. New responsibilities and structures call for authority to be moved as far down the organization as possible and for information to be made available to facilitate this. In return, senior colleagues will want to have access to information about what has been done.

We have discussed the way that work is changing and the nature of the organizational response to this. Many are currently running both approaches side by side, with all the tensions and potential for overload which this involves. One solution may be for organizations to spread the cross-boundary working used for new projects to core activities, to include what has been termed 'the day job'. However, organizations may choose to live, for a while, with different ways of working for different activities or in different parts of the organization. While this will continue to cause strain, it will provide the opportunity to learn from new approaches and for them to be adapted to meet particular needs.

Giving appropriate rewards for change may feel difficult in cash-starved public sector bodies. However, while most people report that more money would be helpful, above all they want to feel that they can make a difference and to have some sense of how they are doing. Involving users potentially brings staff closer to why they came into the public sector and increased authority provides them with more opportunity to make a difference.

New ways of 'seeing' organizations

Gareth Morgan, in his book *Images of Organizations*, identifies a series of metaphors for organizations. He argues that the most powerful has been that of the machine:

> The mechanistic mode of thought has shaped our most basic conceptions of what organization is all about. For example when we talk about organization we usually have in mind a state of orderly relations between clearly defined parts that have some determinate order. Although the image may not be explicit we are talking about a set of mechanical relations. We talk about organizations as if they were machines and as a consequence expect them to operate as machines: in a routinized, efficient, reliable and predictable way.

> (Morgan, 1986)

We are then disappointed when they do not! The machine metaphor is useful in illustrating much of what does and should happen in parts of the public sector. However, as Morgan suggests, it is also a limiting mind set, the more so because it is often outside our conscious thought.

Morgan offers a set of alternative metaphors, including those of brains, organisms, cultures, political systems, psychic prisons, flux and transformation and instruments of domination. Each enables managers to see their organizations in different ways and therefore, to see the limitations of any single metaphor. While the alternatives are no more 'true' than the image of a machine, they offer useful insights into ways of doing things that might be possible if we were not 'machine-bound'. For example, one alternative metaphor, used by Morgan is that of the organization as a brain. If an organization is seen as a brain, we see the importance of interactions with the environment. It becomes clear that discoveries may come from the bottom-up rather than being imposed top-down. It becomes essential not only to help staff learn from their environment, but to wire that learning into the whole organization. This is a very different mindset from wondering how to control from the centre everything that is happening at the edges.

Many organizations claim to be or to aspire to being 'learning organizations'. This would fit well with the brain metaphor. However, while most organizations are relatively good at learning about deviations from system norms or expectations, they are poor at learning whether the norms were correct in the first place. Major barriers exist to this 'double loop learning' within most organizations. These include the fragmentation of information arising from traditional departmental structures; the hidden assumptions that underpin most professional and managerial decisions and what Chris Argyris has called 'defensive routines' used to protect our self image (Argyris, 1990). These make it hard for those inside the organization to challenge the norms which underpin systems and behaviour. Those outside the organization, users and other stakeholders are more likely to be able to provide this challenge if provided with a structured framework for doing so.

If we challenge our mindsets, by using alternative metaphors for our organizations, we reveal what we had taken to be facts of life as hidden assumptions. This allows us the freedom to experiment with new assumptions and therefore new solutions to the problems of organization design. We can begin to rethink 'users' and the public, and their roles within organizations. We might turn the organization inside out, and put the user at the centre. Users can play a role in that thinking, challenging our assumptions, and helping us to 'see' what we do to and for them in different ways.

Work on the culture

As well as learning new ways of seeing, it helps for all managers and staff to work on the existing culture, exploring it, learning to recognize it, facing the problems and patterns in 'the way we always do things here', surfacing the assumptions and behaviours that get in the way. What we can call 'culture-work' is often seen as removed from 'real work' but, in fact, it is vital in helping to identify and remove barriers to change. There are many processes and techniques that can be used, including 'culture audits', 'challenge groups', organizational raids, exploratory project teams and learning sets and so forth. It can help to use drawings, photos and images of different kinds to break out of the 'diagram culture' of the machine, and find different ways to explore how the organization feels. The technique is less important than the fact that ordinary members of staff and managers are involved, and feel confident and safe in identifying problems and working on solutions.

'Unlearning'

Linked to work on the culture, there may be a need for investment in 'unlearning' processes by which individuals can explore the assumptions they have built up through almost unconscious 'social learning' (see Thompson and McHugh, 1995). These might be the assumptions they have built up about service users, or sections of the community, or assumptions they make about other professionals. It can be helpful to work on a day-to-day basis in teams that include people with other professional backgrounds, or those who are 'outside' professional worlds. Professional knowledge and expertise will become more and more valuable as the world becomes more complex, but each profession nevertheless tends to have 'blind spots'. Training and working with practitioners and community leaders from different backgrounds can create opportunities for developing 'creative tension' between the different perspectives and arriving at solutions that are richer than each profession would reach in isolation; as well as providing opportunities to 'unlearn' unhelpful and self-limiting assumptions.

Developing capacity

At the same time, organizations will need to increase their capacity to cope with new ways of doing things. Some of this can be done through recruitment, and recognizing the value of recruiting people from diverse backgrounds with different perspectives, including selecting people who form part of the local community. Simultaneously, existing managers and staff need to keep on learning. An important starting point will be to build understanding throughout the organization about why change is happening, and about the reasons behind user and public engagement. People may need time to build a wider understanding of the changing context, the problems of social exclusion, issues of diversity and racism, as well as changing technologies and lifestyles. If staff understand the reasons for change, they can begin to work out for themselves the new skills and capabilities they need. It will also be important to create organizational support for learning. This means rewarding learning, making space for it, ensuring managers encourage and create opportunities for learning and, making sure that day-to-day work is carried out in a way that encourages reflection and exploration. Managers and staff will want to try out new skills, experiment and practise new ways of doing things in ways that are relatively safe. If the organization wishes to encourage innovation and risk-taking, then it needs to create incentives for doing so. Capability goes beyond simply acquiring new skills; it includes building the confidence of managers and staff to diagnose emerging problems and giving them the autonomy they need to tackle them without panicking and retreating back into tradition!

We believe it helps to work with managers and staff to build agreement about the sorts of skills and competencies that will be needed, and to engage them in designing a development process that will help them to acquire those competencies. That may involve traditional training, but it may also involve reading, working with others, finding ways of learning and practising new competencies at work, coaching, mentoring and work-shadowing, and also ensuring that the support and challenge mechanisms are in place to encourage learning and provide opportunities for individuals to reflect and re-plan. This might also involve regular self-assessment or 360° feedback from managers, peers and employees against agreed competencies as the basis for providing a personal development plan.

The example below is taken from a competency framework drawn up by a group of the most senior managers in a local authority. They worked collectively to explore the future into which they were trying to manage, and then mapped out the competencies they believed they would need to respond. Working together to produce the framework created a good basis for agreement about the development process that would follow.

Managing innovation and improvement

Monitors the environment, competitors, other district councils
Explains change drivers and builds support for organizational response
Benchmarks current performance against best practice
Creates an environment of debate, new ideas, critical assessment and continuous improvement
Enables appropriate experiments and risk-taking
Evaluates innovation against desired outcomes

Providing external focus

Community
Selects appropriate methods and creates an effective dialogue with local people
Acts as an advocate and champion of the local community
Responds to what is heard from the community
Helps colleagues understand and explore community needs

Users
Takes a customer perspective
Creates opportunities for self and staff to learn about and respond to user views

Members
Builds effective relationships with councillors
Works with councillors to achieve organizational goals

Partners
Builds partnerships with other agencies to achieve organizational goals
Facilitates, brokers and negotiates effective partnership working

---

Personal competencies

Achievement orientation
Is outcome-focused
Generates and communicates a clear vision of what needs to be done
Has a positive and optimistic approach
Is proactive and willing to take reasonable risks
Balances demands on time and is focused on priorities

Team working
Collaborates with colleagues,
Works effectively in teams across the council
Influences people outside the line management role
Shares information, encourages communication and builds trust
Builds confidence and participation
Explains options and choices

Personal impact
Values self and is aware of own strengths and weaknesses
Gives feedback and support to others, mixing encouragement and challenge
Reviews own performance
Seeks feedback
Responds well to criticism, not defensive but open to challenge and to change
Is open and honest, shows integrity
Provides credible explanations for decisions where necessary
Values people and listens to their views
Sets a good example and is polite to all

Innovation and creativity
Generates new ideas and encourages others to do so
Is aware of what is happening elsewhere and brings in new ideas from outside
Makes suggestions, encourages discussion, values contributions
Creates space for new thinking
Is unafraid to make mistakes or to be vulnerable
Shares information and concerns
Is receptive and responsive to new ideas

Managing change – preparing for public and community engagement

Local Authorities need a strategy to create an organization which is capable of delivering the level and kind of user involvement they want. This will need to be flexible because once started the process will have an impact on what needs to be done and people will learn from their experiences. However, it will probably need to include the areas covered below.

The first step will be a process of explanation throughout the organization or department. This will involve sharing the reasons for change, and giving staff an opportunity to explore these, express doubts, have them listened to and help build possible solutions. It will be important that change is not seen as a fad or fashion, or simply for the sake of change. It is also important to value what was done in the past as being appropriate for the past. Without this recognition a lot of staff find it difficult to let go of the past and move on. Many of those who work in the public sector will only embrace change if they can see that it is for the good of the organization and for the local people it serves.

The second step will be to help staff explore how things could be in the future, and to build their own confidence and capacity to engage with external pressures for change and plan a response. This can be done through environment scanning, scenario planning techniques, workshops, hypotheticals, simulations or other action learning events. It can help to engage users or members of the public in the processses of thinking through how things might be different if the organization became more user-focused. The need for regular reflection and learning is important as engagement progresses and lessons emerge. Providing people with space and a process to reflect on what is happening and then building this into the normal practice of the organization has often proved key in helping organizations to learn from the past and build capacity for the future.

There is also an important stage in involving staff in preparing well for effective public consultation, including thinking about communication, publicity, informing staff, liaising with councillors, working with the local media, planning the feedback and response strategies in advance, making sure that the time and resources allocated are sufficient to do things properly. Training may need to take place well in advance to ensure that the organization responds well.

Finally, there may be a need to invest in community capacity-building. Members of the public are not automatically skilled at any of the aspects of working with service providers. They need an opportunity to learn these skills. Exactly what they need will, of course, depend on the nature of their involvement and on their past experience. At the most basic, it might involve help with making contacts, personal development, group formation, administration and move on to planning, building networks and negotiation skills.

The Community Development Foundation (1996) has identified the following broad areas where public agencies and local authorities can support users:

- sharing information, for example on how the authority works;
- sharing contacts;
- sharing skills;
- recognizing community organizations have a role to play.

Failure to give help in these areas inevitably leads to frustration with users for not responding 'appropriately'.

Matching organizational change to the organization's stance on user involvement

Finally, it is important to remember that form follows function. So, it is important not simply to introduce random organizational change, but to match the changes carefully to the needs of the stance chosen on user involvement. The more ambitious the strategy of engagement, the more radical the change that will be needed.

If we return then, to the framework for exploring different methods of engagement set out in Chapter 2, we can see that the implications for organizational change can be explored using the set of dimensions outlined on page 158.

As shown in Table 9.2, what will be an appropriate organizational design will depend upon what type of user involvement is envisaged.

In using the grid to consider what organizational changes are necessary, there are two important issues of 'fit' to be considered. The first is inherent in the grid itself, that is that the organization design element 'fits' the stance of user involvement chosen. For example if an organization chooses to support users of a particular service, the roles and responsibilities of the staff involved need to reflect this. Similarly, it is important that the organization design variables 'fit each other', so that, for example, the competencies available or being developed match the chosen job design.

In principle, each cell within the grid could have a different 'solution'. In practice, however, it will make sense to find the minimum number of internal changes that can reinforce each other and create 'critical mass' to support and sustain change. The easier, and the more straightforward change feels, the more likely it is to stick. It will be important to integrate any change to match user engagement strategies with changes planned for other reasons. 'Best value', 'community planning', work on outside initiatives such as 'education action zones' or 'new deal', all need to make sense when taken together – and to solve, not exacerbate, overload problems.

It helps to recognize that changing the organization is hard, and that there will be many setbacks. Sometimes, there will be good learning that tells you the change is not going to work, and something else needs to happen. The application of common sense is always important. The organizational changes explored in this chapter will not be the last, and it will be important to build organizational capacity to become comfortable with a process of continuous improvement. However, experience tells us that routine engagement of service users and members of the public offers a vital perspective that can help to ensure 'good change'. The creation of user-led organizations offers valuable help in responding to the wider pressures that local authorities will inevitably face.

Table 9.2 The organizational design consideration for different levels of involvement

Level of User Involvement/Organizational Design Considerations	Giving Information	Consultation/ Listening	Visioning/Innovating	Judging/Decision-making	Supporting Community decision-making
purpose or mission					
strategy					
roles and responsibilities					
structure					
information and decision-making					
reward systems					
competencies, skills and knowledge					
leadership culture					

10 Conclusion: where do we go from here?

Sue Goss and Kai Rudat

The world of local government managers never stands still, precisely because they stand at the crossroads where people's lives meet government action – constant change is inevitable. However, some changes are longer-lived than others. The current preoccupations within local councils – best value, mayors, new scrutiny arrangements, Beacon Status – are all relatively time-limited means to more serious ends.

'Managing with the public' will require sustained change over many years, but will fundamentally change what public managers do. It is not simply a government 'fad' or a fashionable 'technique'. Relationships between government and people are changing and will continue to change in the future.

Influential social scientists such as Anthony Giddens suggest that we are moving towards a different balance between government and people – where government makes fewer decisions on our behalf, where decision-making is negotiated, rather than imposed, and as members of the public we expect to be listened to. Government at local, national and regional level may increasingly see their role not as acting on behalf of the community, but as orchestrating the actions of the community – negotiating between different sections of the community, brokering compromise and building consensus. Technical and professional knowledge will be as essential – perhaps more essential– as the technology of our world becomes more complex. However, it will be important to inform and educate a decision-making public, not to substitute for them. What does this mean for local government managers facing decisions about user consultation and public engagement?

The most important implication is that this is a field of work that is evolving.

Over the next few years, local government managers will need to draw on and manage a much richer pattern of public involvement than they have been used to in the past. We have explored, throughout this book, the widening repertoire of methods, and local government managers will be expected to become more familiar with all of these, and gain confidence in choosing the right approach in the right circumstances. We are suggesting that the argument about the 'best method' should be abandoned. Increasingly, public engagement will become a flexible production process, as part of the mainstream of service delivery, responding to the needs and preferences of different audiences in different situations. In many cases it is not a single approach, but the right combination – leading from understanding, through dialogue, to effective decision-making. As we have suggested, local managers will want to invent and design approaches that match unique local circumstances.

The second implication is that public expectations of involvement will change. Members of the public will gain knowledge about what is effective and what is not. They will form judgements about the sorts of consultation process they value, which will shape their commitment to participate. We have an increasingly sophisticated and design-conscious audience, which has high expectations of the experiences offered to them as part of their leisure time. Families that we may want to engage in conversation about council services will have experience of TV audience participation, or radio phone-ins. They will go to Thorpe Park, EuroDisney and Center Parcs. They are used to the communication skills of Virgin, Sainsbury's and Marks & Spencer. They have become used to the interactive exhibits in the Science Museum, or the Museum of Moving Image. They will not welcome shoddy process, bad communication or poor design. Increasingly, as we talk to members of the public about their criteria for participation they ask 'Will it be interesting?' 'Will it be any fun?'

The public may come to expect accountability. Increasingly, there is a pressure on local councils not simply to consult, but to show how decisions were made as a result of consultation. Active citizens want to know about the evidence base for decisions, and to be convinced that the decisions were based on the consultation that was carried out. We may need to be prepared to offer an 'audit trail' for big public decisions – to demonstrate both the logic and the evidence that led to them. This does not mean that politicians and managers cannot disregard the views of the public – they may have good reasons to do so. However, those reasons are as much a part of the consultation and dialogue as the decision itself – they will need to be persuasive to those who were listened to, and whose advice was not followed. There will be increasing transparency of decision taking. The introduction of mayors and scrutiny panels may put far more decisions within the public domain, and lead to a revival in the almost dead art of local investigative journalism. Councils will increasingly have to 'prove' they listened, and show how they managed the consequent tensions and dilemmas to achieve social results. These pressures will influence the choice of processes for engaging the public, since simple surveys or 'snapshots' do not provide participants with the information they need to make informed judgments, and so build up problems of raised expectations, wish-lists or unrealistic choices. The use of more deliberative methods enables participants to confront and work through the choices and dilemmas that face the council, and build workable solutions.

Old approaches to 'managing with the public' often saw service users as a problem. The old joke 'This would be a great school if it wasn't for the pupils' is only funny because we have all caught ourselves thinking like that. Managers have allowed fears about raised expectations and unmeetable demands to crowd out their exploration of the more exciting possibilities that public engagement brings. Instead of seeing the people within our communities as 'difficult customers' we can begin to see them as a vast untapped resource. 'We can draw on emerging methods of visioning, discovery and experimentation' described by Anne Bennett, and to model the very processes that build self-confidence and self-respect. Members of the public, whatever their lifestyles or problems, have ideas and energy to contribute. As Loraine Martins and Clive Miller show, we can engage people in innovation and service redesign in ways that break down the 'active professional–passive recipient' relationship that reinforces social problems. Some of the most exciting work, using theatre, art, comedy, cartoons and poetry, begins to break down the barriers between analysis and solution and between planning and action. By living through new ways of doing things, and sharing ways of seeing the world, people – both members of the public and professionals – begin to change.

None of this will be easy. There will be tensions to be managed, and local councils will need to develop the capabilities and frameworks needed to manage them. In Chapter 8 we looked at issues of empowerment. It is important not to underestimate the discomfort that arises when good professionals and committed politicians are faced with people in the community who are angry, and dismissive, or simply apathetic and cynical. It is tough to manage the process of hearing conflicting voices. It is exhausting to work with members of the public that are bullying or abusive. However, it is also exciting and fascinating to learn from people whose lives are very different from ours – to work alongside young people preparing a play about their lives, or to work with Bangladeshi women planning ways to make better use of health care.

Some of the toughest changes will be inside organizations. Local authorities are not prepared for the learning that takes place, and cannot respond rapidly. Organizational change to make space for public engagement will be jerky and discontinuous. There will be many false starts, but as we create more open, reflective and creative organizations, gains begin to reinforce each other. We have seen, in many local authorities, the breakthrough point reached when change can accelerate. It needs to. The gap between the traditional local council and civil society on the brink of the millennium is very wide.

In the short term, there are many dilemmas that cannot be 'solved' but must be 'managed into'. There will be tensions between departmental and corporate working, between single agency and partnership working, between the cultures of public and private sector ways of doing things and between different professional viewpoints about 'the right thing to do'. There will be inevitable territorial warfare, and political bottom lines. Throughout this book we have urged ambition, but we have stressed pragmatism. It will be important to work with the grain of the local culture and local needs, and not to import fancy solutions that do not fit. It will be important to understand, and work within, the complex sensitivities of all the major stakeholders. It will be important to challenge, but also important to celebrate small successes. We can begin to see emerging paradoxes which will require attention by national, regional and local policy-makers, as well as by local government policy-makers.

The first is a growing tension between short- and long-term agendas. Local government managers feel under pressure to achieve immediate results and improvement in performance, sometimes in ways that drive an obsessive focus on day-to-day delivery, with a feeling that any investment in understanding and responding to the changing future is 'a waste of time'. In the new climate of best value, it will be important to embark upon 'best value consultation', and initiatives to engage with the public should be subject to the same 'value for money' scrutiny as all other activities. This manifestly does not mean refusing to look at customer needs and views if we know services are dangerously out of date. We will need a robust, long-term understanding of value. On the one hand, then, the best value regime insists on greater user consultation and involvement. On the other hand, managers feel that space and time for innovation is squeezed by constant pressure on resources. Reconfiguration that could lead to savings often requires upfront investment. Political and managerial leaders at local level will need to build organizational strategy that balances short-term performance against long-term evolution and change. The government can also help by ensuring that monitoring and evaluation systems reward long-term rather than short-term investment.

The second paradox will be driven by advances in technology. The development of TV and telephone voting, set-top boxes and increasing access to the Internet makes it possible to consult a vast number of people in an instant, through the flick of a switch. It would be easy to post a question to thousands of households through community TV stations with the early evening news, and evaluate the answers next morning. Computer-generated surveys will be fast and offer vast coverage. However, this breakthrough comes just as we begin to realize the value of face-to-face conversations, and 'rich talk' and deliberation, and see the potential of community workshops to build friendships and break through isolation. The increasing use of computers to gather opinion would leave out a small but vital section of the community – the technologically poor, who are traditionally the most isolated from decision-making; old people; people without literacy skills in English; people who are ill, or who have no settled home. New technology offers new opportunities, but it could also shut off some of the greatest potential benefits of working with the public to create social inclusion. Used well, however, technology can begin to link depth and breadth of conversation. At the Office for Public Management, we have found that pensioners can be taught to use computers and gain huge advantages from the widened horizons. Hand-held sets can be used to speed up deliberative processes by analyzing and pooling decisions as people work together. The challenge will be to use new technology to strengthen the best aspects of engagement.

Perhaps most important of all, then, any process of engaging with the public must involve active learning; to understand what is going right and wrong; to ensure mistakes are not repeated; and to disseminate and share the insights and analysis that is drawn out. Much of the knowledge inside local authorities and in local communities is tacit, and goes unnoticed and unrewarded.

The challenge of the next few years will be to find ways to exchange learning, not simply within organizations, but between organizations, and between organizations and communities. Job swaps, secondments, learning laboratories, practice-exchange workshops and problem-solving conferences will all help. The work of the I&DeA (Improvement and Development Agency), the LGA (Local Government Association), the Social Exclusion Unit and government departments can help to spread best practice nationally. However, there will be a place for local and regional exchange of learning, perhaps involving parish councils, or youth workers, local businesspeople and local professionals to build up the knowledge and capability in a town or village. In addition, as well as celebrating success, we should learn to celebrate the 'heroic failures' that teach us how to do things differently next time.

Further reading

GENERAL

AMA (1994) *Getting Involved: A good practice guide for councils in the 1990s*, AMA

Arnstein, S (1971) A ladder of citizen participation in the USA, *Journal of the Royal Town Planning Institute*

Beresford, P and Croft, S (1993) *Citizen Involvement: A practical guide for change*, Macmillan, London

DETR (1999) *Achieving Best Value through Public Engagement*, University of Warwick

Gaster, L et al (1999) *History Strategy or Lottery: The realities of local government/voluntary sector relationships*, Improvement and Development Agency (I&DeA)

Goss, S and Ledbeater, C (1998) Civic entrepreneurship, Demos

Sargeant, J and Steele, J (1999) *Who Asked You? The citizens perspective on participation*, Improvement and Development Agency (I&DeA)

INTRODUCTION

PMF (1997) *The Glue that Binds: the public value of public services*, PMF

CHAPTER 1   THE REASONS FOR CHANGE

DETR (1998) *Mordernising Local Government: local democracy and community leadership*, University of Warwick

Pollitt, C (1988) Bringing consumers into performance measurement: concepts and constraints, *Policy and Politics* **16** (2), pp 77–87

CHAPTER 2   CHOOSING A METHOD

Burns, D, Hamilton, R and Hoggett, P (1994) *The Politics of Decentralization: revitalizing local democracy*, Macmillan, London

Gaster, L and Taylor, M (1993) *Learning from Consumers and Citizens*, Local Government Management Board (LGMB)

Local Government Information Unit (1995) *Consulting and Involving the Public*

Local Government Management Board (LGMB) (1997) *Involving the public*

Lowndes, V *et al* (1998) *Enhancing Public Participation in Local Government*, DETR

MacFarlane, R (1993) *Community Involvement in City Challenge*, NCVO

National Consumer Council (NCC) (1994) *Consulting Your Users: A handbook for public service managers*, King's Fund Centre, London

Stewart, J (1995) *Innovation in Democratic Practice*, Institute of Local Government Studies, Birmingham

Stewart, J (1996) *Further Innovation in Democratic Practice*, Institute of Local Government Studies, Birmingham

CHAPTER 3   SURVEYS AND ENGAGEMENT

For a reference text on approaches to designing and conducting surveys, see:
Czaja and Blair (1996) *Designing Surveys*, Pine Forge

Oppenheim, A N (1992) *Questionnaire Design, Interviewing and Attitude Measurement*, Pinter, London

For general information about user and citizen consultation, with special reference to survey and panel research, see:
Alexander, J *et al* (1996) *Doing User Surveys: A research methods handbook*, London Borough of Islington

DETR/Local Government Centre (1999) *Achieving Best Value through Public Engagement*, Warwick Business School

DOE (1993) *Tenant Feedback: A step by step guide to tenant satisfaction surveys*, DOE

Hatton, P (1990) *Survey Research for Managers: How to use surveys in management decision making*, Macmillan, London

How to Consult Your Users (1999) Service First Unit Publications/Cabinet Office

Local Government Association (1999) *Panels in Practice – Conference Papers*, Local Government Information Unit, Cabinet Office, LGA

Local Government Information Unit (1997) *Citizens' Panels: A new approach to community consultation*

Local Government Information Unit (LGIU) (1995) *Consulting and Involving the Public*

Local Government Management Board (LGMB) (1997) *Involving the Public*

Parston, G and Cowe (1998) *Making the Connections: Citizens mapping the big picture*, Public Management Foundation, London

CHAPTER 4   INVOLVEMENT IN DELIBERATION AND DECISION-MAKING

Coote, A and Lenaghan, J (1997) *Citizens' Juries: Theory into practice*, IPPR

Fishkin, J (1995) *The Voice of the People: Public opinion and democracy*, Yale University Press

Hall, D and Stewart, J (1997) *Citizen's Juries in Local Government*, LGMB

Social and Community Planning Research (1999) *Citizens' Juries: An appraisal of their role based on the conduct of two women only juries*, Cabinet Office, London

Stewart, J (1999) *From Innovation in Democratic Practice towards a Deliberative Democracy*, Institute of Local Government Studies, Birmingham

Yankelovich, D (1991) *Coming to Public Judgement*, Syracuse University Press

CHAPTER 5   QUALITY MANAGEMENT: DELIGHTING THE CUSTOMER

Beckhard and Harris (1997) *Organizational Transitions*, Addison Wesley, Harlow

Byham and Cox (1991) *Zapp! The Lightening of Empowerment*, Century Business, London

Crosby, PB (1979) *Quality is Free*, McGraw-Hill, New York

Deming (1996) *Out of the Crisis*, MIT/CAES

Evans (1994) The human side of business process re-engineering, *Management Development Review*, 7 (6)

Hall, Rosenthal and Wade (1994) How to make re-engineering *really* work, *The Mckinsey Quarterly*, no 2

Harrington (1991) *Business Process Improvement*, McGraw-Hill, New York

Harvey, J (1996) ISO 9000 – is it worth the investment? *Update, British Council Newsletter*, June

Harvey, J (1998) Achieving best value through service process redesign, *Policy Research and Management*, Autumn

Juran, JM (1979) *Quality Control Handbook*, McGraw-Hill, New York

Oakland, (1991) *Total Quality Management*, Butterworth-Heinemann

Redman, Snape and Wilkinson (1995) Is quality management working in the UK? *Journal of General Management,* **20** (3) Spring

Robson, M (1980) *The Journey to Excellence*, Wiley, New York

Robson, M (1993) *Problem Solving in Groups*, Gower, Aldershot

Von Oech (1992) *A Whack on the Side of the Head*, Viking, London

CHAPTER 6   BUILDING A COMMON VISION OF THE FUTURE

The following is not an exhaustive list but does include the breadth of approaches, their origins and key practitioners in the field.

Asch, S (1952) *Social Psychology*, Prentice-Hall, New York

Bunker, B and Alban, B (1997) *Large Group Interventions*, Jossey-Bass, San Francisco

Emery, F E and Trist, E L (1973) *Toward a Social Ecology*, Plenum, New York

Jacobs, R W (1994) *Real Time Strategic Change*, Berrett-Koehler

Owen, H (1992) *Open Space Technology – A User's Guide*, Abbott Publishing

Pratt, J *et al* (1999) *Working Whole Systems*, Kings Fund Centre, London

Walker, P *Participation Works – 21 techniques of community participation for the 21st century*, New Economics Foundation, Centre for Community Visions, London

Weisbord, M (1992) *Discovering Common Ground*, Berrett-Koehler

Sources of help and advice

Colbourne, L and colleagues at Projects in Partnerships, London (0171 407 8585)

Democracy Network (Local Government Association and Local Government Management Board)

Democratic Practice: A guide (1998) LGA Publications, London

McMahon, L and colleagues at the Office for Public Management, London (0171 837 9600)

CHAPTER 7   WORKING WITH LOCAL COUNCILLORS

Budge, I (1996) *The New Challenge of Direct Democracy*, Blackwell, Oxford

Fishkin, J (1991) *Democracy and Deliberation: New directions for democratic reform*, Yale University Press

King, D and Stoker, G (1996) *Rethinking Local Government*, Macmillan, London

Modernizing Local Government

Mulgan, G (1994) *Politics in an Antipolitical Age*, Polity Press, Cambridge

Phillips, A (1994) *Local Democracy: The terms of the debate*, Commission for Local Democracy

Young, K and Rao, N (1997) Public attitudes to local government, in Hambledon *et al, New Perspectives on Local Governance*, Joseph Rowntree Foundation

CHAPTER 8   EMPOWERING THE DISEMPOWERED

Croft, S and Beresford, P From paternalism to participation: involving people in social services, *Journal of the Market Research Society*, **38** (3), Open Services Project and Joseph Rowntree Foundation

Dowson, S (1991) *Keeping it Safe – Self-advocacy by people with learning difficulties and the professional response*, Values into Action

Goss and Miller (1995) *From Margin to Mainstream: A study of user involvement in community care*, Joseph Rowntree Foundation

Hart, R (1992) *Children's Participation, from Tokenism to Citizenship*, UNICEF

Phillips, E (1993) *Consultation – I thought we did that last year: consultation with black and minority ethnic groups in the preparation of community care programmes*, London Research Centre

Prasha, U and Shan, N (1986) *Routes or Roadblocks? Consulting minority communities in London Boroughs*, Runnymede Trust

Sills, A and Desai, P (1996) Qualitative research amongst ethnic minority communities in Britain, *Journal of the Market Research Society*, **38** (3), pp 247–65

Taylor *et al* (1992) *User Empowerment in Community Care: Unravelling the issues*, School for Advanced Urban Studies

User Centred Service Group (1993) *Building Bridges between People Who Use and People Who Provide Services*, National Institute of Social Work

Winn, L (ed) (1990) *Power to the People, The key to responsive services in health and social care*, Kings Fund Centre

CHAPTER 9   CHANGING THE ORGANIZATION TO BE EFFECTIVE AT USER ENGAGEMENT

Report of the Commission on Social Justice (1994) *Performance through capability*, IPD

Impact of People Management Practices on Business Performance, IPD paper no 22

Argyris, C (1990) *Overcoming Organizational Defences*, Prentice Hall, Hemel Hempstead

Community Development Foundation (1996) *Building Community Strength*

Doyle, P (1994) *Marketing, Management and Strategy*, Prentice Hall, Hemel Hempstead

Handy, C (1994) *The Empty Raincoat*, Hutchinson, London

Morgan G (1986) *Images of Organizations*, Sage, London

Senge, P M (1990) *The Fifth Discipline*, Century Business, London

Skelcher, C (1993) *Public Money and Management*, July–September

Tarplett, P and McMahon, M (1999) *Managing Organisational Change*, Office for Public Management

Tarplett, P and Parston, G *Managing Strategy*, Office for Public Management

Thompson, P and McHugh, D (1995) *Work Organisations: A critical introduction*, Macmillan, London

Index

Visit Kogan Page on-line

Comprehensive information on
Kogan Page titles

Features include

- complete catalogue listings,
  including book reviews and
  descriptions

- on-line discounts on a variety
  of titles

- special monthly promotions

- information and discounts on
  NEW titles and BESTSELLING titles

- a secure shopping basket facility
  for on-line ordering

- infoZones, with links and
  information on specific areas of
  interest

PLUS everything you need to know
about KOGAN PAGE

http://www.kogan-page.co.uk